© Swedish Environmental Protection Agency, and the authors, 1998

ISBN 91-620-1180-4

EDITOR AND CONCEPT: Peter Hanneberg

AUTHORS: Rolf Löfgren, Peter Hanneberg and authors listed in table of contents

PROJECT MANAGER, PUBLISHING SECTION: Sonja Arnell

TRANSLATORS: Al Burke, Martin Naylor, Anna Paterson (pp. 95–96, adapted)

MAPS PP. 6, 15, 23, 71, 129: Hans Sjögren

DESIGN: Tomas Löckert, IdéoLuck AB

REPRO AND PRINTING: Fälths Tryckeri AB, Värnamo, April 1998

PAPER: Silver Blade 150 g, chlorine-free

ADDRESS FOR ORDERS: Swedish Environmental Protection Agency, Kundtjänst, SE-106 48 Stockholm, Sweden

TELEPHONE: +46-8-698 10 00

FAX: +46-8-698 15 15

E-MAIL: kundtjanst@environ.se

HOME PAGE: www.environ.se

Sweden's National Parks

PETER HANNEBERG   ROLF LÖFGREN

HM King Carl XVI Gustaf in Tyresta, Sweden's 23rd national park, for the opening ceremony in September 1993.

THE NATURAL LANDSCAPES OF SWEDEN have a grandeur and diversity in which every Swede can take real pride. The interest in our country's clean environment and natural beauty which I often encounter is clear testimony to the excellent reputation enjoyed by these unique assets, not only here at home, but also abroad.

My travels around Sweden, in both an official and a private capacity, afford me many welcome opportunities to experience at first hand the variety and richness of the country's scenery and wildlife. The flower-filled deciduous woodlands of the south offer an exciting contrast to the majestic mountains and desolate mires of Lapland, the dense, moss-carpeted virgin forests of the interior and the open islands of sand or granite off our coasts.

In recent years I have opened a succession of new national parks up and down the country. I have done so with great pleasure, since they represent something very close to my heart, our beautiful and unspoilt natural environment and its invaluable biological diversity.

Thanks to this form of protection, later generations will I hope also be able to enjoy our unique natural heritage. Beyond price, it belongs not only to us, but also to the future.

HM KING CARL XVI GUSTAF

In May, the alternating red and yellow blooms of elder-flowered orchid make a striking spectacle on Ängsö, a national park since 1909.

Sweden's National Parks

Sweden's national parks listed by year of
designation, 1909–96, with details of their
areas. Asterisks indicate that the park in
question was later extended once (*)
or twice (**), as shown lower down the
list, where the present area is given.
In the case of Stora Sjöfallet, however,
the area was reduced to enable a
hydroelectric scheme to be built.

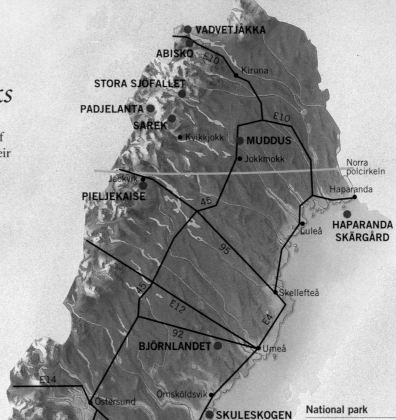

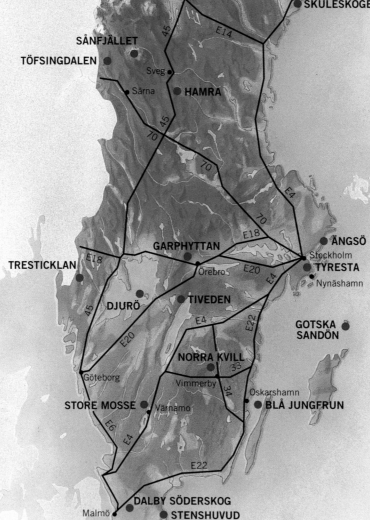

National park	Year designated	Area, hectares
Abisko	1909	7,700
Garphyttan	1909	111
Gotska Sandön**	1909	(368)
Hamra	1909	29
Pieljekaise*	1909	(200)
Sarek	1909	197,000
Stora Sjöfallet*	1909	(139,800)
Sånfjället*	1909	(2,622)
Ängsö*	1909	(73)
Pieljekaise (extension)	1913	15,340
Dalby Söderskog	1918	37
Stora Sjöfallet (reduction)	1919	127,800
Vadvetjåkka	1920	2,630
Blå Jungfrun*	1926	(66)
Norra Kvill*	1926	(27)
Töfsingdalen	1930	1,615
Muddus	1942	49,340
Padjelanta	1963	198,400
Gotska Sandön (extension)	1963	(3,648)
Store Mosse	1982	7,850
Tiveden	1983	1,352
Skuleskogen	1984	2,950
Stenshuvud	1986	302
Sånfjället (extension)	1988	10,440
Gotska Sandön (sea area included)	1988	4,500
Blå Jungfrun (sea area included)	1988	191
Ängsö (sea area included)	1988	188
Björnlandet	1991	1,130
Djurö	1991	2,400
Tyresta	1993	1,970
Norra Kvill (extension)	1994	111
Haparanda Skärgård	1995	6,000
Tresticklan	1996	2,909

Number of national parks in 1997: 25
Area in 1997: 642,295 hectares

Contents

Deciduous woodland in Dalby Söderskog, which was declared a national park in 1918.

Preface

TWENTY-FIVE NATIONAL PARKS have now been established in Sweden, and more are on the way. Our country can boast a very wide range of valuable and attractive natural areas. The national parks comprise the best and the most representative of them, from the majestic landforms of the north to the gentler deciduous woodlands of the south. Their variety and beauty are impressive, as is their conservation value from a scientific point of view.

The national parks of the mountains are the wildest and most spectacular, with their alpine peaks and vast open spaces, lush valleys and vivacious streams and rivers. Wildernesses of gigantic proportions, but at the same time areas which the Sami have used for reindeer herding for centuries.

It should not be forgotten that the country's national parks are intimately bound up with the history of their local communities, as well as containing natural assets which the whole nation has an interest in preserving for future generations. The parks are therefore of significance not only for nature conservation, but also from the viewpoint of local history and culture and for tourists from both Sweden and other countries.

The development of a network of national parks representative of the country's characteristic or unique landscape types is an important element in our nature conservation strategy. We need these parks in order to conserve our ecosystems and biodiversity, and to ensure that both we and future generations can enjoy and be inspired by an unspoilt natural environment.

The purpose of this book is to draw attention to the treasures which the national parks of Sweden represent and to encourage many people to visit them – with due care and respect. The Environmental Protection Agency hopes that *Sweden's National Parks* will help to create a greater awareness of and feeling for this our priceless natural heritage, which we have a joint responsibility to safeguard and maintain.

ROLF ANNERBERG
Director-General
Swedish Environmental Protection Agency

Daisies in flower in a meadow at Stenshuvud in Skåne. The management plan for this national park includes livestock grazing. The park was opened in 1986.

National parks
– a legacy to our children

*"The Creator has clothed the whole world in a
tapestry of flowers, and placed Man upon it to
walk, to live and to find pleasure there."*

ELOQUENT WORDS, SPOKEN by perhaps the most famous Swede
in history, Carolus Linnaeus. During his lifetime, 1707–78, Linnaeus
laid the foundations of systematic botany and zoology, which were
to endure for centuries to come. But for all his pioneering efforts in
science, he was also the poet who could not help including, in his
morphological descriptions, references to the sensuous and aesthetic qualities of nature. It was he who, in Sweden, sowed the seeds
of an ecological view of nature, the idea that all phenomena form a
functional part of a larger whole. This eighteenth-century thinker
often pondered the question:

*"Is, then, every single created thing
created not merely for its own sake,
but rather for the sake of other creatures?"*

To some extent, the view of nature that now prevails is a Linnaean
legacy. While searching for new objective knowledge about individual species or about how people could best benefit from them,
Linnaeus also created a feeling for nature which lives on in the
Swedish national consciousness. He inspired an interest in the
natural environment from which, much later, our national parks
would be born. The fundamental ecological outlook which gradually evolved has assumed considerable significance in modern
nature conservation, and hence also in the management of the
country's national parks.

This holistic view of the environment in which we live was
captured in a few pithy lines by the popular Swedish writer Tage
Danielsson (1928–85):

*"Every time you protect a tree, an albatross,
a river, that is threatened with destruction
– you are protecting yourself."*

❦

SWEDEN'S NATIONAL PARKS Through this book, which combines
facts with personal experiences, the Swedish Environmental Protec-

tion Agency wishes to provide an introduction to this country's
national parks.

Our presentation centres on the assets – the biological diversity,
the representative landscapes, the scientific and aesthetic features –
which we are anxious to safeguard. Factual texts describe the varying
characters of the parks, their scenery, flora and fauna, history and
main attractions.

These descriptions are then set in a framework of first-hand
encounters with nature – what we see with our eyes and perceive
with our senses when we visit these gems. Direct images of their
landscapes are conveyed by both personal impressions recorded by
eleven Swedish writers and photographs taken by leading nature
photographers.

HISTORY At the time of writing (1997), Sweden has 25 national parks,
and around ten more are planned. But let us look back at how it all
began. It was in the United States, where, in 1872, an area in the Rocky
Mountains by the name of Yellowstone was set aside as a "national
park". For a long time after that, Yellowstone was to serve as the
famous prototype for this form of protection. On our side of the
Atlantic, the Swedish polar explorer Adolf Erik Nordenskiöld sug-
gested in 1880, shortly after his celebrated voyage through the North-
East Passage on the Vega, that a corresponding form of national
protection should be introduced for the wilderness areas of Sweden
and her Nordic neighbours.

Another three decades were to elapse, however, before Europe's
first national park was established. In 1904, Swedish MP Karl Star-
bäck tabled a parliamentary motion on the subject, to be followed in
1907 by a report criticizing "man's ruthless encroachments" on
nature, which were "dictated by his impulsive greed".

This concern resulted, on 25 June 1909, in the Swedish Parliament
passing a Nature Protection Act which established a legal basis for the
designation of national parks. The same year it was decided that nine
parks were to be created in Sweden, the first in Europe. The virgin
forest of Hamra, the cultural landscapes of Garphyttan and Ängsö,
one-tenth of the island of Gotska Sandön in the Baltic Sea, and the five
mountain areas of Abisko, Pieljekaise, Sarek, Stora Sjöfallet and
Sånfjället were chosen as the country's first national parks.

Subsequent progress in Sweden was relatively slow. A further
eleven national parks were set aside, at fairly long intervals, up to

1986. With the entry into force of a new Nature Conservation Act on 1 January 1965, the focus of modern, long-term planned protection of the natural environment shifted to the nature reserve. Since then, a large number of nature reserves, and also nature conservation areas and wildlife sanctuaries, have been established.

In 1976, the National Environmental Protection Board (set up in 1967, later the Environmental Protection Agency) took over responsibility for the country's national parks from the National Forest Service. Since then, the Agency's Natural Resources Department, headed by Rune Frisén, has endeavoured to identify the areas and features of greatest conservation interest in Sweden and a series of new national parks have seen the light of day. King Carl XVI Gustaf, well-known for his commitment to nature conservation in various contexts, has presided over their opening.

NEW NATIONAL PARKS PLAN

Earlier this century, national parks were set aside in a fairly haphazard fashion, on the basis of their aesthetic or tourist appeal. As a result, the park network did not live up to the requirements which this form of protection is nowadays expected to meet. It was heavily biased towards the mountain landscapes of the north, while archipelago areas, for instance, were not represented at all and several of the areas in the south were small.

In 1989 a new, credible platform for the creation of further national parks was established when the Environmental Protection Agency presented its "National Parks Plan for Sweden", describing what the country's national parks system should look like in the years to come. The new system is intended to make systematic use of the strong protection afforded by national park status, with a view to safeguarding Sweden's most valuable natural areas for the future.

⸻

The criteria for the creation of national parks in Sweden are that they should
- be established by Parliament on land belonging to the state,
- be outstanding or distinctive examples of their landscape types, contain natural assets of great value, or be of particular scenic interest,
- incorporate entire landscape units, normally covering at least 1,000 hectares,
- consist predominantly and in their core areas of natural countryside of an undisturbed character,
- together be representative of widespread or unique Swedish landscape types, in a system spread across the country, and
- be capable of being effectively protected and at the same time being used for research and outdoor recreation without impairing their natural assets.

OUR NATIONAL HERITAGE

National parks constitute a country's legacy to future generations. Part and parcel of the concept is the idea that the entire nation must assume responsibility for their protection. The population at large exert their influence through parliament and central government, which directly control national park designations.

The high status that attaches to a national park also attracts greater attention, both nationally and internationally. Parks are expected to incorporate the most outstanding, representative and attractive portions of a country's remaining areas of undisturbed nature. The actual protection given to habitat types and species, though, does not differ very much from that provided by nature reserve status.

Sweden's 1989 National Parks Plan proposed 20 new parks, as well as recommending that the boundaries of some existing parks should be redrawn or extended and that others should lose their national park status. Since then (up to 1997), five of the new national parks proposed in the plan have been established and one has been extended. The Environmental Protection Agency's aim is to put the rest of the plan into effect within the next ten years.

NATIONAL PARKS WORLD-WIDE

The creation of national parks and other protected areas is an important component part of the wide-ranging field of global environmental protection. The need for active nature conservation has evolved in parallel with the overall development of human societies.

Criteria for the selection and management of national parks have been drawn up by the World Conservation Union (IUCN, founded in 1948), in collaboration with the United Nations Educational, Scientific and Cultural Organization (UNESCO). They are broadly the same as the Swedish criteria just mentioned, which are based on Sweden's Nature Conservation Act. Lists of and statistics relating to the world's national parks and other protected areas are published regularly, and national parks congresses are held every ten years.

National park designation is now the most widespread form of protection of outstanding natural areas. Of the 170 countries included on the 1994 UN list of protected areas, 130 had established national parks. Over the last 25 years, the total extent of national parks and other protected natural areas has increased from two million to almost ten million square kilometres.

Europe can boast some 200 national parks. In the world as a whole there were 2,041 national parks in 1993, covering 3.8 million square kilometres, i.e. over nine times the area of Sweden. They made up around 40 per cent of the total area of protected nature world-wide. The 25 national parks created in Sweden up to 1997 cover 6,423 square kilometres, which is 17 per cent of the area of

A light Nordic summer's night at Ramsojaure. Muddus in Norrbotten was designated a national park in 1942.

The view from Sarektjåkkå, 2,090 m above sea level, takes in the most imposing landforms in Sweden. Sarek was one of Europe's first national parks, set aside in 1909.

*"As soon as I came up onto the mountains,
it was as if I had been granted new life
and a heavy burden had been taken from me."*

CAROLUS LINNAEUS (1732)

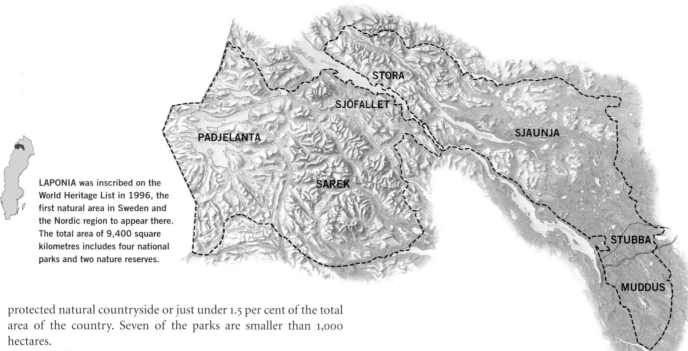

LAPONIA was inscribed on the World Heritage List in 1996, the first natural area in Sweden and the Nordic region to appear there. The total area of 9,400 square kilometres includes four national parks and two nature reserves.

protected natural countryside or just under 1.5 per cent of the total area of the country. Seven of the parks are smaller than 1,000 hectares.

Sweden has 1,693 nature reserves (1 January 1997), with a combined area of 27,493 square kilometres. The number of national parks and nature reserves in the country with an area exceeding 1,000 hectares is 214. Protected natural areas cover a total of 37,109 square kilometres, just over 8 per cent of the area of Sweden. This includes nature conservation areas and wildlife sanctuaries, as well as areas with small-scale habitat protection.

LAPONIA – A WORLD HERITAGE SITE In December 1996, the largest and most valuable continuous area of wilderness in Sweden and Europe was honoured with an international protected status higher even than that of a national park. Following a joint nomination by the Swedish Environmental Protection Agency and the Central Board of National Antiquities, UNESCO's World Heritage Committee inscribed the Laponian Area – consisting of the Sarek, Padjelanta, Stora Sjöfallet and Muddus National Parks, the Sjaunja and Stubba Nature Reserves and a number of smaller areas adjacent to the parks – on the World Heritage List. Previously, in 1967, three of the constituent parks, Sarek, Muddus and Padjelanta, had been awarded the Council of Europe's European Diploma.

The Laponian Area covers no less than 9,400 square kilometres. Glaciers, mountain heaths, birchwoods, mires, lakes, coniferous forests and rivers – the entire spectrum of northern Swedish inland habitat types is represented in this exceptional area. To date, this is the only Natural World Heritage property in the Nordic region, and it is almost five times larger than Sweden's biggest single national park (Padjelanta).

OUR LEGACY TO THE FUTURE "All but a small handful of countries have national parks. The challenge facing nations today is no longer deciding whether conservation is a good idea, but rather how it can be implemented in the national interest and within the means available in each country."

Those words were written by the Brundtland Commission in 1987. In the long term, the protection of natural resources will be crucial to all forms of development. The purpose of national parks is to set aside particularly significant sections of the ecosphere within which we live. Actually protecting these areas in practice will be an exercise in showing the sort of respect for living things which is necessary to our own survival. Every time we protect life, we protect ourselves.

"There is still time to save species and their ecosystems. It is an indispensable prerequisite for sustainable development. Our failure to do so will not be forgiven by future generations."

The words of the Brundtland report contain a timeless truth. And it is this truth which is guiding the Swedish Environmental Protection Agency in its efforts to create new national parks and manage them for the future.

As we have seen, Linnaeus, in the eighteenth century, was one of the first Swedes to begin to appreciate the fundamental interrelatedness of nature. His thoughts on "sustainable development", over two hundred years before the term was coined, are now more relevant than ever:

"I do not even rightly know how the world could without difficulty remain in existence if but a single animal species upon it were to be lost."

PETER HANNEBERG   ROLF LÖFGREN

Abisko

Abisko National Park is a place of many delights, including a birch-clad valley, flowery alpine meadows and dazzling river rapids. The park is surrounded on three sides by lofty mountains and, in the north, by Scandinavia's largest alpine lake, Torneträsk. Abisko is easily accessible and has long been a popular starting point for hikes in the mountains of Lapland.

LANDSCAPE Abisko National Park is comparatively small, and is located far up in of northern Scandinavia's majestic mountain range, which stretches south from Lake Torneträsk to Mt. Kebnekaise. Abisko is a Saami (Lapp) word that means "Ocean Forest", a reference to the nearby Atlantic.

The combined effects of the sheltering mountains and the nearby ocean result in an unusual local climate. Abisko Valley lies in the rain shadow east of the high mountains and has the lowest precipitation in Sweden, only some 300 millimetres annually. Visitors can experience the Arctic's 24-hour daylight and, during eight weeks of summer, observe the midnight sun from the park's highest point.

From its highest level, the Abisko Valley descends to Lake Torneträsk, fifteen kilometres to the north. Over that distance, the Abiskojåkk Brook drops 150 metres and terminates in a beautiful waterfall into a deep canyon of two kilometres' length. With its 20-metre-high vertical walls, the canyon is the national park's most dramatic feature.

Abisko is at its most beautiful on clear, still September days, when the lakes reflect the bright colours of the birchwoods and the mountain heath.

Included in the park are the eastern slopes of mounts Njulla and Slåttatjåkka, all the way up to their crests which are 1200 metres above sea level and 850 metres above Lake Torneträsk. A small section of Lake Torneträsk also lies within the park. From the top of Mt. Njulla there is a magnificent view of the lake's broad waters and the mountain landscape, with the familiar U-valley of Lapporten to the east and high massifs to the south and west.

The bedrock of Abisko Valley consists of hard shale in alternating light and dark layers that are especially distinct in the canyon. There are also some deposits of yellowish "Abisko marble", a dolomite which shows traces of the quarrying that once took place along the upper reaches of the brook.

VEGETATION The renowned plant life of Abisko National Park results primarily from the lime-rich bedrock of Mt. Njulla. The mountain birch forest on the slopes of Mt. Njulla consists of exceptionally fertile wooded meadows with such flowering plants as wood cranesbill, globeflower, angelica and baneberry. Some sections of the forest floor are carpeted in ferns, especially the ostrich fern.

During the 1950s and '60s, large areas of the Abisko Valley's birch forest were infested by larvae of the geometrid moth. Over half of the older trees died, and their decaying white snags remain standing today. This natural disturbance of the ecosystem will be a distinctive feature of the park well into the future. Despite the fact that Abisko is located far west of the normal boundary for coniferous forest, several sparse stands of short, broad, older pine trees rise like sentinels above the birch forest in the sun-warmed valleys. In recent years, the pines have managed to regenerate themselves, and new stands are now growing up.

Scattered about the birch forest of Abisko Valley are sub-alpine

> *"A lake is the eye of the landscape, reflecting the essentials in its depths."*
> ALBERT VIKSTEN (1956)

heaths, open areas that are believed to be the result of ground frost and soil displacement which hinder the growth of a permanent ground cover. Delicate species, many of them rare, are able to establish themselves on the newly-formed surfaces. They begin to bloom in May, starting with purple saxifrage and continuing with alpine butterwort, Arctic rhododendron (Lapland rosebay), bog rosemary and moss campion. These are followed during the height of summer by yellow saxifrage, mountain avens and the national park's rarest plant, the Lapp orchid, for which this is the only known site in Sweden.

ANIMAL LIFE The most conspicuous mammals of the park are its moose (elk), which are present mostly during the summer. Common birds of the mountain birch forest include the willow warbler, brambling, fieldfare, redwing, tree pipit and redpoll.

In those tracts of birch forest which have been ravaged by geometrid larvae dwell birds that nest in tree-holes, including the willow tit, redstart and lesser spotted woodpecker. The melodious bluethroat can be heard throughout the birch forest and the park's rarest small bird, the Arctic warbler, may be sighted on the slopes of Mt. Njulla.

There are also large numbers of ducks and wading birds; they are most prevalent on the heaths, near the smaller lakes, and in the little delta where the Abiskojåkka River empties into Lake Torneträsk. Nesting species include the whimbrel, golden plover, greenshank, red-necked phalarope, wigeon and common scoter. Among the birds of prey which nest in the park are the merlin, rough-legged buzzard and, especially during abundant lemming years, short-eared and hawk owls.

The Abiskojåkka has carved a deep path through the strata of "hard schist", a type of mylonite.

THE HUMAN PRESENCE The Saami people have long made use of the Abisko area, which is part of the Rautasvuoma Saami Village's summer grazing range. The national park includes a reconstruction of a traditional Saami dwelling place.

Abisko has for many years also been a popular setting for scientific research and mountain recreation.

The lights in the windows of the Swedish Touring Club's mountain station at Abisko counterbalance the meagre twilight of the Arctic winter.

The Lapp orchid is a rare species, with Abisko its only Swedish site.

The male whimbrel often stands guard in a tree while the female sits on the nest, and can attack intruders so ferociously that even ravens have to accept defeat.

The golden petals of the yellow wood violet light up the surrounding greenery.

Arctic rhododendron. Linnaeus discovered this species in the mountains on 8 July 1732 and at first thought it was an azalea, but later assigned it to the genus *Rhododendron*.

Foundation	The national park was established in 1909, in order to preserve a northern Scandinavia mountain area in its natural state.
Location	South of Lake Torneträsk, ca. 100 kilometres northwest of Kiruna in Norrbotten County.
Area	The park contains 7700 hectares (19,027 acres), of which 6700 are land and 1000 water surface. Of the land area, 3900 hectares consist of mountain birch forest, and 2800 hectares alpine heath.
Attractions	The view from Mt. Njulla. The rich flora. The Abiskojåkka River canyon and waterfall. The park's nature centre.
Visiting Abisko	The national park is easy to reach by train or car from Kiruna or Narvik. At Abisko there are hotels and cottages, as well as a nature centre with an exhibit on the park's natural history. There is also an aerial cable car to the top of Mt. Njulla. The national hiking trail, Kungsleden ("King's Way"), begins at Abisko, running south through the park and on toward Mt. Kebnekaise.

For the protection of nesting birds, the Abiskojåkka River delta is off-limits to visitors from May 1 to July 31 every year.

Part of the now protected virgin forest of Björnlandet. A path leads to the top of Björnberget, from where there is a good view of Lake Angsjön. Beyond the park boundary, commercial forestry continues.

Björnlandet

Björnlandet is a protected remnant of the pristine forest that greeted the first human inhabitants of Norrland. The lovely ancient pines, the marshy spruce forest draped in beard-lichen, and the traces of past forest fires combine to make Björnlandet a dynamic, living ecosystem, as well as a biological archive that discloses the dramatic events of bygone times.

LANDSCAPE Rolling hill terrain is the most common type of landscape in Sweden, stretching in a broad belt from the south-central region of Värmland to central Västerbotten in the north. There, it is succeeded by the flatter, marshy landscape of the monadnock plain (a broad plateau with scattered conical hills). Rolling hill landscape, which is also found in southern Sweden, contains relatively little marshland and is almost entirely covered in evergreen forest.

> *"This past summer the people here, in the east and the west, were engaged in quenching forest fires. It was exceptionally dry at that time: the fires spread with incredible speed, and in all quarters they were preceded, surrounded and followed by fear, anxiety and alarm. The smoke hung like a thick cloud over the whole of southern Lapland."*
>
> J. W. ZETTERSTEDT (1832)

Björnlandet is located among the steep hills that form a boundary between Ångermanland and Lapland. Until recently, this sparsely populated region included large roadless areas and tracts of well-preserved forest. Björnlandet is a remnant of that

New citizens of the spruce forest, five young, wide-awake Tengmalm's owls.

located near the hiking trail in the eastern section of the park.

Deep in Björnlandet's southern valley lies Ångsjön, the national park's only lake. The valley also holds the park's only large marsh complex, consisting of gently inclined fens and a few string bogs. In addition, there are several smaller marshes and watercourses distributed throughout the park.

VEGETATION Despite some logging activity during the past two centuries, a large portion of Björnlandet remains untouched, and retains the strikingly beautiful aspect of primeval forest. Pine is the dominant species, including some exceptionally old and broad-beamed trees. The most ancient living trees are 500 years old; but in most parts of the forest, there are dead trees, snags, and fallen trunks with even earlier origins. Some of these have been preserved by pitch and resin, and may well have begun their lives during the Viking Era over a thousand years ago.

The forest of Björnlandet has been greatly influenced by fire. Charred stumps and scorch marks on living trees bear witness to the extent of past forest fires. There have been at least ten major fires since 1665, and they have actually benefitted the pines which, due to their thick park and lofty crowns, are able to survive even intense fires. The spruces, on the other hand, were best able to survive in damp hollows. Providing a sharp contrast to the dense primeval spruce forest are the sparse, dry stands of pine where the effects of past fires are very evident.

As a result of the meagre soils and the comparatively harsh inland climate, Björnlandet has a fairly insignificant flora that is typical for this forest region. Lichens, heather, crowberry and bilberry are the most common plants in much of the park. The brook ravines and marsh woods are more biologically diverse habitats, with ferns, horsetails, alpine sowthistle, wood cranesbill, wintergreen and twinflower.

Also found in the marsh woods are the Lapland buttercup and the lesser twayblade orchid, as well as some species of mushrooms and lichens that grow on wood.

ANIMAL LIFE The park's animal life is also characteristic for this part of Sweden. Bear and lynx occasionally wander through the park, while the moose, pine marten, mountain hare and red squirrel are quite common. Typical bird species include the capercaillie, brambling, Siberian jay and goldcrest. Other resident species include the three-toed, black, and grey-headed woodpeckers, the pygmy and Tengmalm's owls, and the hazelhen.

THE HUMAN PRESENCE There has probably never been a resident population in Björnlandet. It is only at the park's eastern border that traces of human settlement have been found. In some areas, there are stumps left behind from the selective logging conducted at the turn of the century. The logs were floated down Ångsjö Brook, in which there still can be seen historically interesting remnants of old logging dams and wood pilings.

Along with the rest of Lapland, the national park has for centuries been used for reindeer herding, and is today part of the North Vilhelmina Saami Village's winter grazing land.

Quiet Lake Ångsjön mirrors a summer-blue sky. Hay was once cut on the nearby mires.

ancient forest, having escaped the impact of modern logging.

Björnlandet National Park includes some ten distinctive hill-crests and a large bowl-shaped valley with a lake at its southern extremity. The park's highest elevation is 550 metres, and the maximum rise from valley floor to hillcrest is 200 metres. Steep cliffs up to 70 metres in height contribute to the dramatic profile of the national park's terrain.

A striking feature of the area is the large number of boulders scattered about. There are also several waterlogged hollows containing boulders that have been raised and shifted by the action of ground frost. A large boulder-filled hollow of nearly two hectares is

In early spring, the display call of the capercaillie can be heard in the undisturbed pine forest.

The lushest vegetation is to be found on damp slopes.

Lesser twayblade, one of the few orchids of the coniferous forest, is pollinated by hoverflies.

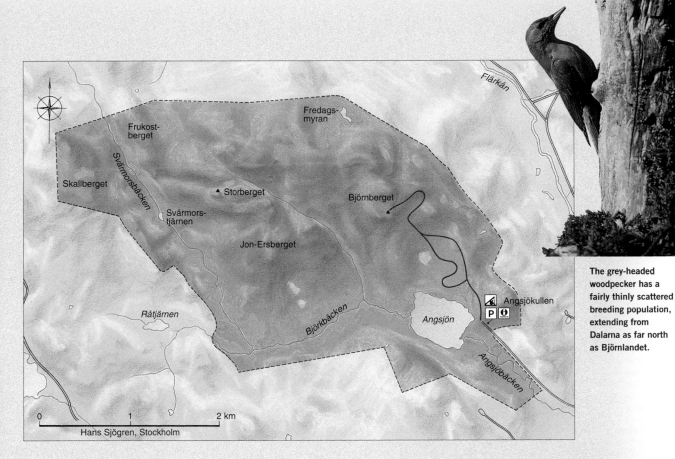

Hans Sjögren, Stockholm

The grey-headed woodpecker has a fairly thinly scattered breeding population, extending from Dalarna as far north as Björnlandet.

Foundation	Björnlandet National Park was established in 1991, in order to preserve a valuable and representative area of rolling hills and primeval forest in its natural state.
Location	Twenty kilometres southeast of Fredrika in the Municipality of Åsele, Västerbotten County.
Area	1130 hectares, including 35 hectares lake surface. The land area consists of 990 hectares coniferous forest, 100 hectares marshland and five acres of boulder-strewn clearings.
Attractions	The primeval forest, e.g. along the hiking trail between Lake Angsjön and Mt. Björnberget. The view from Mt. Björnberget. The boulder grounds.
Visiting Björnlandet	The national park can be reached most conveniently via the road between Fredrika and Åsele. A side road some ten kilometres south of Fredrika goes to Fjälltuna and the Flärkå River. The last stretch goes across the river to Lake Angsjön at the park's eastern boundary, where there is a wind shelter and information display. From this point, a hiking trail leads through the primeval forest and up Mt. Björnberget.

The pine marten is rarely spotted, even though it occurs throughout Sweden, including in Björnlandet.

Blå Jungfrun

Rising in lonely majesty from the waters of Kalmar Sound is Blå Jungfrun, a bald rock dome with a high "forehead" of the reddest granite. The isolated island has served as a seafarers' landmark for centuries, and its unusual ecosystem has long attracted students of natural history. Among the earliest recorded visits was that in 1741 of Carl von Linné, the 18th-century botanist who established the modern system of species classification.

LANDSCAPE Blå Jungfrun keeps its lonely watch in the waters between the southern mainland and the flat limestone island of Öland, but has little in common with either. The island is a unique geological formation— an isolated dome of red granite that rises to a height of 86 metres above sea level and 130 metres from the seafloor. By comparison, the loftiest islands of the Baltic archipelagos reach only half as high.

"It is said that all the witches come here (in truth, quite an arduous journey) every Sheer Thursday; but that anyone who has once set foot in this place never travels here again, and certainly there are grounds for this fable; for if any place in the world looks frightful, this surely is one of the cruellest."

CAROLUS LINNAEUS (1745)

The reddish colour of Blå Jungfru comes from the potassium feldspar in its rock of rapakivi granite. Rapakivi is a Finnish word that means "crumbling stone", a reference to the fact that the rock's large crystals easily erode to gravel. Nevertheless, the ice-worn rocks of Blå Jungfru are unusually smooth and free of cracks. Along the northern shore, there are some sea stacks and cave formations created by the forces of weather and waves. On the southern shore are two fissure grottoes, named Jungfrukammaren and Kyrkan ("Maiden's Chamber" and "Church").

The island's granite dome has a rounded form. Its northern half is dominated by smooth-worn rock outcrops that rise upward in a series of steps to the summit at the island's centre. Southward from the summit, the terrain is more dramatic, with a cliff that plunges into a broad-leaved wood and nearly to the water's edge. Otherwise, the southern part of the island is fairly level, and is covered in trees and shrubs.

Blå Jungfru has been shaped by the ice ages of the past two million years. The rocks on the north side of the island have been worn smooth, and most of the loose material has been washed away. On the south side, the glaciers dislodged stones and boulders which were then left behind in crevices and on ledges. Also found here are graceful mounds of stone rubble, and a thin layer of soil that provides favourable conditions for the dense vegetation.

VEGETATION Nearly two-thirds of Blå Jungfrun's surface consists of rocks that lack higher forms of vegetation. The flora of the remaining third is surprisingly rich and diverse. Birch and dwarf willow grow in hollows in the island's northern sector. Near the summit there is a sparse, wind-lashed wood of pine and birch. The level, boulder-strewn terrain of the southern sector has a distinctly different character, with a shady wood of oak along with the odd maple and linden (lime). After his 1745 visit to the island, Carl von Linné reported that, "Its groves were so dense that anyone without an axe could hardly penetrate them".

A striking feature of the oak wood is the ivy that grows thick on the boulders and high up in the trees. The ivy has been damaged by past fires, as well as by the rabbits that were introduced around the

Opposite: **As early as 1555, archbishop and historian Olaus Magnus mentioned a rock in the sea which sailors had christened "The Maiden" in order to "avoid ill omens and storms at sea".**
Below: **With its rapakivi granite, the island could just as well have been called "The Red Maiden".**

Like the crown of a royal head fashioned from red granite, with its lofty brow and verdant woods behind, Blå Jungfrun rises from Kalmarsund.

middle of the 19th century. But since the rabbit population was wiped out by the exceptionally cold winters of the early 1940s, the island's vegetation has recovered and is once again approaching the density that Linné described.

Otherwise, the oak wood has a diverse flora, with such species as woodruff, coralroot bittercress, black pea and angular Solomon's seal. All told, over 200 species of vascular plants have been discovered on the island. However, the national park is best known for the rich diversity of lichens that grow on its ledges, boulders and tree trunks.

In the glistening red rock pools, algae provide the complementary colour green.

ANIMAL LIFE As a result of the island's isolated location, barren landscape and steep shoreline, relatively few animal species are represented. Mountain hares and bats are the only mammals. The most characteristic bird species is the black guillemot, which nests among the boulders along the southern shore of the island. Other nesting species include velvet scoter, eider, rock pipit, stock dove and several small woodland birds.

THE HUMAN PRESENCE According to local folklore, Blå Jungfrun is the mythical "Bald Mountain" where witches congregate on Halloween. The Swedish chronicler, Olaus Magnus, noted as early as 1555 that sailors had dubbed the island "Jungfrun" ("The Maiden") in an attempt to mollify the wrath of the sea. Laid out on a flat ledge is a very interesting historical artefact, a large stone labyrinth known as a "Trojan fortress". It was already in place when Linné visited the island in 1741, and may have been the work of seafaring people.

Other famous Swedish visitors include the poet laureate, Werner von Heidenstam, whose 1896 wedding feast was held on the island; among the guests were such fellow celebrities as the poet Gustaf Fröding and the painter Albert Engström.

In all likelihood, Blå Jungfrun has never had a resident population. But in 1904 there began a period of quarrying, in the course of which the island's most remarkable giant potholes were blown to pieces. After World War I, powerful voices were raised in support of protective measures. Through a donation from engineer Torsten Kreuger, the island was purchased and turned over to the crown, and subsequently protected with the status of national park in 1926.

Stretching to the south of Blå Jungfrun's red crown is a tangle of deciduous woodland.

Kalmarsund

0   100   200   300 m
Liberkartor, Stockholm

A conspicuous feature of Blå Jungfrun's bird life is the black guillemot, a lively species that can easily dive to depths of 25 metres.

Foundation	The national park was established in 1926 in order to preserve the island in its natural state.
Location	In Kalmar Sound, between Oskarshamn and northern Öland, in the Oskarshamn Municip., Kalmar County.
Area	Blå Jungfrun has 66 hectares (163 acres), of which sixteen hectares consist of broad-leaved woods, ten hectares of pine woods, one hectare of mixed woods, and 39 hectares of bare rocky terrain. The national park also includes the surrounding waters to a limit of 300 metres from the shoreline, for a total land-and-water area of 191 hectares. The island is 1150 metres long and 840 metres wide.
Attractions	The smooth, reddish granite rocks that have been ground and polished by glaciers. The dense broad-leaved woods. The view from the island's summit. The stone labyrinth. The fissure grottoes.
Visiting Blå Jungfrun	In calm weather, there are one-day boat tours to the national park from Oskarshamn on the coast, and from Byxelkrok on Öland. There is a marked trail through the forest, along the west shore and up to the summit.

Black pea, which thrives on rocky ground, grows in the island's oakwoods.

"Here one could see no trace of man, save only a labyrinth, a Trojan fortress, made of small loose stones laid upon a rock, no doubt by some seaman delayed here by a contrary wind" (Linnaeus, 1745).

Dalby Söderskog

Dalby Söderskog is the most exceptional grove of broad-leaved trees on the fertile plain of Skåne. It is a mature and somewhat unusual wood, with an impressive display of spring flowers, dense summer foliage and ardent birdsong. It is also undergoing a transformation as a result of both natural processes and the human impact on the surrounding landscape.

LANDSCAPE The flat landscape of southwestern Skåne has been profoundly influenced by agriculture and human settlement. Grazing land is scarce. Trees and shrubs are generally restricted to farms, tree-lined roads, and ancient marl-pits. The dense broad-leaved grove of Dalby Söderskog is an unusual feature of the Skåne plain, and had already attracted the interest of nature conservationists by the beginning of this century.

"In the bare April woods, waiting for the sun,
a magic carpet already covered the ground,
for anemone and violet together wove
a star-like pattern, the beholder to astound.

Yellow star of Bethlehem and pink corydalis
spread among the thickets their gossamer cloak,
following the tussocks in chill proximity
to the beads of spray from the rushing brook."

ANDERS ÖSTERLING (DEDICATED TO DALBY)

The national park is situated on an extremely fertile Baltic moraine, the lime-rich soils of which are several metres deep. The moraine was formed during the last ice age and is not completely level. In the hollows, there are a number of shallow fens with characteristic vegetation. The park's terrain slopes gently to the southwest, from 75 to roughly fifty metres above sea level. The drop in elevation is evidenced by the brook that winds through the park's eastern section, where it has gouged a deep ravine along its lower reaches.

VEGETATION Dalby Söderskog has felt the influence of humans for a very long time. Its present state is probably the most natural it has experienced since the Middle Ages, when it was used for grazing. Periods of logging and intensive grazing have alternated with less intrusive interludes, during which the wood was able to recover.

All indications are that elm and ash are the most natural tree species for this type of soil. The ancient oaks that remain from the period of intensive grazing, with its open and less shaded conditions, no longer get sufficient light for self-regeneration. Still standing are some giant oaks dating from the early 18th century which have been preserved by the thinning of competing species.

Today, the national park is a mixed wood of elm, ash, oak and beech. Smaller numbers of alder, birch, lime and maple trees are also present. The only homogeneous stands are of beech, which seems to be fairly successful in competing with the elms. But for the most part, it is the elms that have best managed to regenerate themselves in the deep shadows of the grove. In the natural course of events, the dominance of the elms should continue to increase— if the Dutch elm disease that first appeared in the park during the 1980s does not spread much further.

Beneath the high treetops there is a well-developed growth of smaller trees, including hazel, hawthorn, elm and ash. But only in a few places is this intermediate zone dense and compact. Much of the wood conveys the impression of a pillared hall, a very pleasing sight during spring and summer.

In comparison with normal Swedish conditions, Dalby Söderskog has the exotic character of more southerly climes. The rich soil yields an impressive display of spring flowers, such as the wood and yellow anemones that bloom in thick broad carpets, together with lesser celandine and scattered bouquets of yellow star of Bethlehem. A special springtime attraction is the *Corydalis cava*, of which the red and white varieties grow profusely in the southern section of the park. When the leaves of the trees have unfolded and the summer shadows cover the ground, the anemones are replaced by a solid green carpet of dog's mercury and goutweed.

Opposite: **The spring display in Dalby Hage attracts many visitors. Wood and yellow anemones, hepatica, lesser celandine and corydalis bloom below the still-bare trees.** Below: **In winter, the green woodpecker digs beneath the snow in search of ants.**

A fallen tree trunk concealed by moss, amid a summer carpet of dog's mercury, its flowers now faded.

ANIMAL LIFE The park has a rich bird life, with a large number of species that are typical of mature broad-leaved woods in southern Sweden.

The old hollow trees of the park are occupied by starlings, tawny owls, stock doves, and by black, great spotted and green woodpeckers. Among the many smaller birds are the icterine and wood warblers, the blackcap and the thrush nightingale. More than thirty species nest here every year.

THE HUMAN PRESENCE As long ago as the Middle Ages, the wood was used for grazing by the Augustinian monastery in nearby Dalby. Grazing and selective logging continued during the following centuries, to an extent that varied with shifts in ownership between the Danish and Swedish crowns.

A remarkable historical artefact, enclosing half the national park, is a broad and metre-high earthwork whose purpose and origins are obscure. It may have been a defensive structure of some sort.

The pink and white flowers of corydalis dominate Dalby Söderskog in spring.

The name *Corydalis cava*, like the old Swedish name "hollow rootwort", refers to the species' hollow tuberous root. It was once used as a remedy for osteomyelitis and worms.

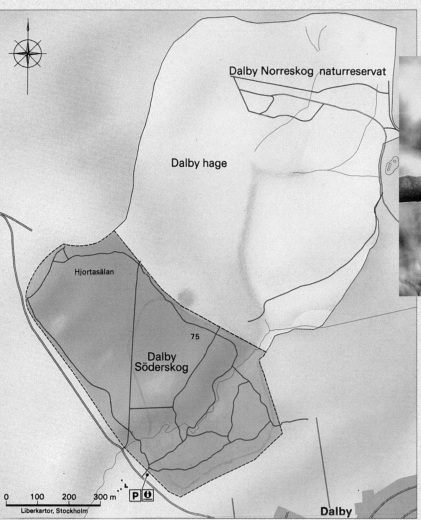

"And the child listens and no doubt thinks, like the oriental emperor of the fairy-tale, that a bird that can sing like that must be very large and beautiful," wrote Swedish author Bengt Berg in 1962, referring to the thrush nightingale.

Lesser celandine flowers in profusion at the same time as wood anemone and hepatica.

Foundation	Dalby Söderskog was established as a national park in 1918 for the purpose of preserving an area of southern Swedish broad-leaved forest.
Location	Approximately ten kilometres east of Lund, in the Municipality of Lund, Skåne County.
Area	36 hectares (89 acres) consisting entirely of mature broad-leaved forest.
Attractions	The lush groves of the broad-leaved forest. The spring floral display. The bird life.
Visiting Dalby Söderskog	The national park is easily accessible by car. Exit from Highway 16 between Lund and Dalby. There is a parking area at the park entrance.

Djurö

Djurö National Park offers a representative sample of the natural features of Europe's largest lake. Few Swedish archipelagos are more remote than this appealing cluster of islands in the midst of Lake Vänern.

LANDSCAPE Vänern is something so unusual as a lake that has the appearance of an open sea. This is evident at the many places along the shore from which the visitor can view an unbroken horizon formed

Opposite: Djurö is an archipelago with a character all its own, offering many quiet encounters with nature on a lake with sea-like horizons.
Below: Djurö's vegetation is limited by its thin soils. Dry pine forests alternate with mires adorned with Labrador tea, but also with rich communities of herbs, particularly on Gisslan.

by the meeting of sky and water. Most of Lake Vänern's islands and archipelagos lie near the shore. But the Djurö Archipelago, lying in lonely isolation far out in the lake's northern basin, is an exception.

The national park consists of some thirty major islands, and as many smaller islets and skerries. The largest and northernmost island, Djurö, has an area of about 150 hectares (370 acres). The other islands form a fairly tight pattern that stretches south and southeast. The bedrock along the eastern flank of the archipelago slopes gradually into shallow waters with skerries and submerged rocks. To the west, however, the shores are steep and the adjacent waters are up to seventy metres deep. The islands are generally low and level, with occasional elevations of up to twenty metres above the lake surface.

The bedrock consists largely of gneiss, which is poor in nutrients. But running across the northern part of Djurö is a vein of greenish amphibolite, which is manifest in a strip of more luxuriant vegetation. The soil layer is thin, and the terrain's basic character is set by the wave-washed rocks along the shores and by the rock outcrops of the island interiors.

VEGETATION The islands' thin moraine soils and the nutrient-poor bedrock impose limits on its plant life. Most of the islands are dominated by pines growing on rocky soil—an attractive type of forest with sparsely distributed, broad-beamed trees. Only the outermost rocks and skerries are completely bare. Here and there are patches of lusher vegetation, with broad-leaved trees and a richer variety of flowering plants. An interesting example of this is Gisslan, the most southerly island of the archipelago, which is essentially a ridge of lime-rich stone rubble. It has a small grove of birch and lime (linden), along with hungry plants such as hepatica, cowslip, lily of the valley and angular Solomon's seal.

Reminders of past human activities on Djurö can still be seen today, in its grassy clearings and broad-leaved trees. In shallow, sheltered waters near the larger islands grow broad expanses of reeds—a typical feature of freshwater archipelagos.

ANIMAL LIFE The isolated location of the Djurö Archipelago has made it impossible for all but a few mammalian species to make their way to the island and sustain themselves. The northern water vole and a few bat species are probably the only naturally occurring mammals. Foxes are able to scurry over the ice from the mainland during the winter. There are some mountain hares, as well as fallow deer which keep the grassy areas open.

Among the birds are typical saltwater species such as the great black-backed gull and the oystercatcher. The greylag goose and osprey nest on the islands; common water birds include the mallard, goldeneye, teal and black-throated diver (Arctic loon). But it is the common tern, herring gull and common gull which characterise the birdlife of the archipelago, by virtue of their sheer numbers.

In the interiors of the tree-clad islands, the bird life is less abundant. Characteristic species of the evergreen woods are the parrot crossbill, black grouse, redwing and woodcock.

In addition to the numerous water birds, the archipelago is known for the many amphibians that thrive in the rock pools, fens and shallow reed beds. Toads, frogs and newts occur in great numbers. Inland, one may come across the slow worm and viviparous lizard. The grass snake is common and, on the larger islands, the adder is also present.

A red-and-white lighthouse stands guard as if this were a sea coast. Djurö's first lighthouse was built back in 1874; the one seen here dates from 1912. Opposite: Striations on Djurö.

THE HUMAN PRESENCE   It is believed that Djurö Island was first inhabited in the middle of the 16th century. Over the years, ownership has alternated between the crown and private individuals. Limited farming on the small patches of arable land, and fishing were the basic means of livelihood. At its zenith, the resident population consisted of four families with a total of some fifteen individuals.

The period of permanent residence came to a close at the end of the 19th century. The islands began to be used as hunting grounds, and a hunting lodge was built. Several new game species were introduced, but only the mountain hare and fallow deer have survived. Djurö was also the site of a lighthouse for nearly a century, from 1874–1969. The lighthouse and keeper's quarters still stand near the harbour of Malbergshamn.

The osprey, a characteristic species of the archipelago, heading for its pine-top nest.

ROLF EDBERG

Djurö – an inland archipelago

Djurö. An island in a small archipelago on Lake Vänern. Its outcrops of rock are chiselled with parallel
grooves. A script to be deciphered, a story to be un-
derstood, the past coming to life in the present. Djurö sums up
the history of this ever-changing lake.

As the great ice sheet receded, it carved its inscription on the
bedrock and emptied its meltwaters into a sea whipped up by
the winds blowing from its edge. The dent in the earth's crust
made by the ice gradually straightened itself out, and large
tracts of sea became land. All that remained was a vast lake.
Vänern was born.

And the striations in the rocks hint that this is not the end
of the story. The submerged ridge with its scatter of islands between Great Vänern and the western part of the lake will one
day surface, dividing Vänern into two completely separate
lakes.

To the south of Djurö, you can make out the pigeon-blue
silhouette of Kinnekulle, to the north, the unbroken expanses
of water that once astonished the writer and restless traveller
Harry Martinson when, as a recent recruit to the crew of the
rusting *Gerda*, he peered out from the boiler room to find there
was no shore in sight.

There is still something of a primeval sea about Lake Vänern, this remnant of an age when once far vaster waters covered
the land. There is a blueness in the air and a trumpeting in the
waves that cross its wide surface, which lays claim to no less
than a seventh of Sweden's far from meagre lake area. In chop-
py conditions, waves lap with an indolent sensuality against the
shores of the island in the middle of this watery realm. In
stronger winds, they pound like sledgehammers against its
western side, where clean-scoured cliffs plunge steeply into the
depths, while the storm-buffeted pines above strain inland,
often grotesquely twisted.

Djurö's eastern shore is a different story altogether: flat
rocks and cobbles, a couple of small, sandy lagoons, and trailing alders to reinforce the feeling of an idyllic inland water. To
the west, the windswept sea coast, to the east, the sheltered lake
shore, all just a kilometre or so apart. Such are the contrasts of
this island.

In the 1970s, the lake was "raked" by special survey ships,
revealing hitherto unknown depths and adding thirteen cubic
kilometres to previous estimates of its volume—it was as if the
contents of the country's third largest lake, Mälaren, had been
emptied into it.

When Vänern's water is smooth, it mirrors the blue skies
above. When it rolls up its sleeves, the waves prove to have a
bronze tinge to them, the stain of humus from the forest soils of
a drainage basin covering a tenth of Sweden's land area. For all
its majesty, for all that it contains a fifth of the country's water,
and for all its thousands of islands and its marine pretensions,
ultimately Vänern is just a forest lake.

The end of the ice sheet was the beginning of life, in a world re-
born.

The heather is in bloom and the summer beginning to fade as
we roam the main island of the Djurö group. The air is filled
with fragrant salves and the whirr of insects. Where there is
some shelter from the westerly winds,
heather and bilberry grow knee-deep.
Scots pine, the centrepiece of the Vänern
basin forests and the undemanding col-
onist of many a poor patch of heath or
rocky ground, sends out roots sometimes
as thick as arms, which twist and turn and
grope their way across the rocks in search of crevices offering
earth and moisture—life's tough, stubborn instinct to survive.

*"There is still something of
a primeval sea about Lake
Vänern, this remnant of
an age when far vaster
waters covered the land."*

In a glade, a surprising scene opens up: a recently abandoned
meadow fringed by spruces, which insist on more fertile soil
than pines. The meadow itself supports a sunlit cluster of oaks,
limes and birches. Beyond it, the pine heath reasserts itself.

That birds should have found their way here seems just as
natural as it was for Darwin's finches to colonize the Galapagos
Islands. It is hard to imagine Djurö without its ospreys, keeping
watch from their pine-top nests, its divers and mergansers, or its
herring gulls skydiving hungrily into the shallows.

But what about terrestrial life—how did it reach a group of islands eight kilometres from the nearest land? The snakes, the lizards, and the frogs which in the mating season are said to fill the
fens with their nocturnal, organ-bellow croaking and puffing?

Three fallow deer bound gracefully across an autumn-yellow

The habitat types found on Djurö are partly of man's making. In 1890 the industrialist Frans Kempe bought the island and built a hunting lodge here. In its vicinity, the landscape became increasingly park-like.

meadow. These antelope of the North call to mind the savannah of warmer climes, but they also provide a reminder of man's involvement behind the scenes.

On Vänern we find the least known—and hence the best preserved—of Sweden's archipelagos. This is particularly true of these islands in the middle of the lake. It was because of their remoteness and their relatively undisturbed state that Djurö and the galaxy of islets stretching away to the south-west of it were declared a national park, the only freshwater archipelago with that status in Europe, and unique even in the global family of national parks.

However, people have lived on the main island since the days of the first of the Vasa kings. From the seventeenth century on, it was handed down from generation to generation in a family of fishermen. In 1890 the archipelago was bought up by the Kempes, forest magnates who introduced mountain hares, roe, red and fallow deer, grouse and pheasants, to turn the islands into a hunting-ground. Photographs show the hunting parties posing with their trophies. But there was little sport to hunting on an island as small as this. All that is left

now is the herd of fallow deer, which keep the meadows grazed in the summer and are regularly fed fresh hay in the winter.

From the sheltered Malbergshamn harbour, marked paths guide the visitor round the main island, well-beaten like forest paths that have since become overgrown and which you can feel with your feet, but not see. So thin and sensitive to erosion is the island's covering of soil that it is best to resist the temptation to deviate from them.

The thirty tiny islands clustered to the south of the main one all have their distinctive character. The calcareous soil of Gisslan, the southern outpost, supports a surprisingly verdant lime grove. But there can be no forays ashore here—most of the groups of islets are bird sanctuaries, where landing is not allowed in spring or summer.

The ringing of the axe is no longer heard on Djurö. Trees which old age finally overtakes are left where they fall, to return to the soil that nourished them.

And so, in the closing years of the twentieth century, new virgin forest is in the making.

Fallow deer were introduced as game in 1912, and now help to keep the old farmland open.

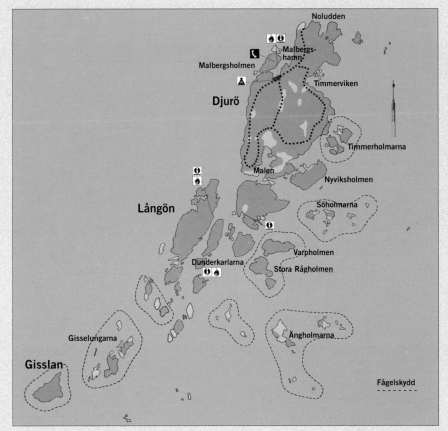

Lilies of the valley spread their sweet fragrance when they flower in May.

Greylag geese nest around the islands of Lake Vänern.

Foundation	Djurö Skärgård National Park was established in 1991, in order to preserve a Lake Vänern archipelago in an essentially natural state.
Location	In the middle of Lake Vänern, 25 kilometres northwest of Mariestad in the Municipality of Mariestad, Skaraborg County.
Area	2400 hectares (5930 acres), of which 315 hectares are dry land; the main island has 150 hectares.
Attractions	The distinctively isolated setting, and the special marine character of a large inland lake.
Visiting Djurö	The Djurö Archipelago can only be reached by means of privately-owned or rented boats. It is easy to land along the northern and western shores, but not via the shallow waters to the east. Along the eastern and southern shores there are bird refuges to which access is forbidden during the nesting season, from April 1 to July 31 every year. There are several good natural harbours, of which the most frequently used is Malbergshamn on the north shore of Djurö Island, where there is an information display. A marked trail makes a circuit of the island.

In spring, the mating calls of numerous frogs resound among the reeds.

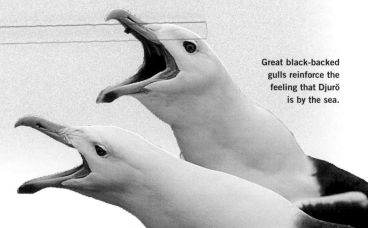

Great black-backed gulls reinforce the feeling that Djurö is by the sea.

Garphyttan

Garphyttan National Park consists of woods and meadows, originally established by humans, that are now spreading over the southern slope of Kilsbergen ridge and down to the Närke Plain. Previously the site of a hill farm, the most valuable features of the park are its human history and its flowery meadows.

LANDSCAPE Situated in the western Närke region, Kilsbergen is a long mountain ridge covered in evergreen forest. The area's iron ore, water power and extensive forests provided favourable conditions for a mining industry that originated in the 14th century. By the 16th century, a large number of mines, blast-furnaces and forges were in operation. The mining industry gave rise to hundreds of small farms and settlements, where the year was divided into a seasonal cycle of farming, charcoal production, mining and iron-making.

"Heaven has landed on a blade of grass; that is why it trembles."
BO SETTERLIND (1983)

Garphyttan National Park incorporates the land and buildings of Svenshyttan's "East Farm" on the lower slopes of the ridge. From the

Left: **This side of the fence, marsh marigolds are a blaze of yellow, while in the wooded meadow beyond spring cowslips are in full bloom. This part of Garphyttan National Park is kept open by traditional haymaking.**
Below: **The hawfinch's powerful bill can easily crush a cherry stone that can withstand a weight of fifty kilograms.**

old farmstead, the ground rises steeply to Svensbodaberget, 210 metres above sea level.

Across the slope runs a distinctive bluff; the nearby ground is strewn with boulders. The presence of limestone in the primeval bedrock is reflected in the rich vegetation at the foot of Kilsbergen.

VEGETATION Garphyttan's luxuriant plant life results from human uses of the soil and forest over several centuries. Establishment of the national park in 1909 marked the start of a development similar to that of Ängsö. At the time, it was erroneously believed that the lovely meadows could best be preserved by leaving them alone. But that policy led to overgrowth of the meadows and a corresponding decline in their floral splendour. It was not until thirty years later that the mistake was recognised. Through the reintroduction of traditional practices and other restorative measures, the park's flowery meadows and broad-leaved woods remain in place as cheerful nooks of Kilsbergen's evergreen forest.

That part of Garphyttan which is now maintained as meadowland was previously used for growing crops. In the small, irregular fields are heaps of cleared stones, along with ash, elm, maple and lime trees of various sizes. The meadows are cut when the flowers stop blooming in July, and leaf-fodder for farm animals is clipped from some of the trees in traditional fashion. Carpets of wood anemone, hepatica and cowslip bloom in the spring. Summer is the time for many other flowers, including columbine, meadow buttercup, globe-flower, wood cranesbill and sticky catchfly. Nearly 300 vascular plants have been identified in the area around the old hill farm.

The only vegetation native to the area is believed to be a stand of ancient pines amongst the rocky outcrops of Svensbodaberget.

Otherwise, the coniferous forest consists largely of spruce imported from Germany; some stands of those trees are now over a hundred years old.

ANIMAL LIFE The animal life of the national park is concentrated mainly in the meadows and broad-leaved woods, where the passionate songs of the blackbird, redwing and song thrush can be heard in the spring. The robin, dunnock and garden warbler are typical smaller birds of the area; the hawfinch and nutcracker also visit on occasion. Other interesting animals of the park are the dormouse, northern birch mouse and smooth snake.

THE HUMAN PRESENCE Up until 1822, East Farm at Svenshyttan was worked by three families, their houses built close together and surrounded by small fields. The rest of the non-forested land consisted of some meadows that stretched far to the south.

After the national reorganization of farm boundaries imposed by the crown in 1824, the little settlement expanded and most of the meadowland was converted to crops. Today, eight acres of that cropland are still being maintained; but of the buildings, only the foundations remain. Other areas of the old farmstead are overgrown with a verdant broad-leaved wood of mixed birch, ash, aspen, maple and elm.

The park's wooded meadows are home to the common dormouse, a species believed to hail from a warmer era.

Sticky catchfly takes its name from the stickiness of its stems.

The sparrowhawk finds plenty to feed on in the varied cultural landscape of Garphyttan.

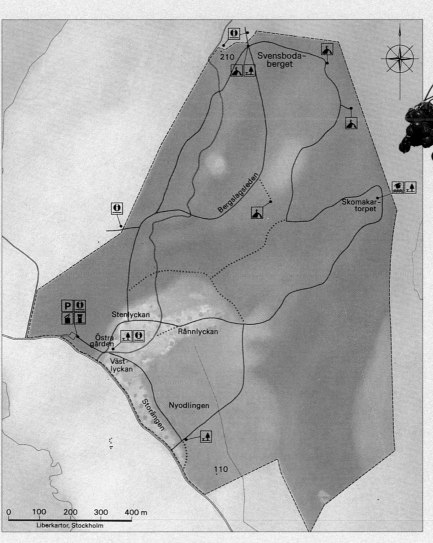

The redwing lingers late into the autumn in Garphyttan's woods and meadows.

The smooth snake is a good climber.

Foundation	The national park was established in 1909 in order to preserve a historic agricultural landscape in essentially unaltered condition.
Location	Roughly twenty kilometres west of Örebro on the slope of Kilsbergen ridge, in the Municipality of Lekeberg, Örebro County.
Area	111 hectares (274 acres), of which 70 hectares are evergreen forest, 26 hectares mixed forest, six hectares broad-leaved wood, eight hectares meadowland, and one hectare roadways.
Attractions	Ancient farmland with a rich array of flowers. The view from Svensbodaberget.
Visiting Garphyttan	A turn-off from Highway E18 west of Örebro leads to Svenshyttan at the park boundary, where there is a parking area. There are two loop-trails, one through the meadow area, the other passing over the crest of Svensbodaberget which offers a superb view of the surrounding area. The regional hiking trail, Bergslagsleden, also runs through the park.

Gotska Sandön

Gotska Sandön is the most isolated island in the territorial waters of Sweden and the entire Baltic Sea. It is remote, desolate and barren, but at the same time strangely beautiful. With its miles of sandy beaches, its dense pine forest, and broad horizons in every direction, Gotska Sandön is a very special place that has fascinated visitors for centuries.

LANDSCAPE   Most of the beaches along the coastline of Sweden's Baltic coast are rocky. But Gotska Sandön, a small section of a sand reef formed during the retreat of the last ice age glacier, is a notable exception. Transported by meltwater to the edge of the ice cap, great quantities of stone, sand and clay were deposited in the sea to form the long and narrow reef.

The Gotska Reef stretches fifty miles north from Fårö Island, just off the northern tip of Gotland. Sandön first broke the surface of the Baltic Sea five thousand years ago and, due to continuing land elevation, its highest point is now 40.3 metres above sea level. In places, the layer of sand over the underlying bedrock is as much as 75 metres deep.

Left: Over twentyfive kilometres of beaches fringe the pine forests of Gotska Sandön.
Below: *Ergates faber*, a five-centimetre long longhorn beetle, in the dead forest.

The island in its present state has been shaped by the forces of wind, wave and current. Large shifting sand dunes have accumulated at Bredsand, Källahamn and Franska Bukten. Further inland are so-called "boundary dunes" which can reach heights of up to seventeen metres. Here, the sand is held in place by sedges, grasses, mosses and lichens, which bridge a narrow gap to the even more binding roots of the interior's pine forest.

The sand on the inland side of the boundary dunes will remain in place indefinitely — as long as the ground cover is not damaged by fire. At several locations in the forest, there are remnants of former dune formations. One such site is Arnagrop on the east side of the island, where a large stand of trees was once smothered by shifting dunes. Those dunes were subsequently removed by the wind, leaving behind a silver-grey battalion of dead trees.

VEGETATION   Given to its simple nature and isolated location, Gotska Sandön cannot sustain a very great diversity of plants and animals. The ground cover consists largely of shoreline grasses and, on the open heaths amidst the pine forest, heather and lichen. The island's vegetation is the result of its extremely dry and sandy environment, which is fascinating in its own right and enhances the visitor's experience of the unusual plant life.

There is a surprising abundance of bird's-eye primrose and marsh helleborine in the damp hollows between the dunes. Two other orchids that grow on the island are the red and narrow-leaved helleborines, from which an interesting hybrid has also developed. The delightful small pasque flower can occur in great numbers, and along the shore can be found sea rocket, prickly saltwort, sea sandwort, and sea holly. The well-maintained meadow near the island chapel is a much-appreciated botanical site.

"Here on Sandön, opposites stand out with such force and clarity that the struggle itself and its fluctuating fortunes dominate everything."

CARL FRIES (1963)

ANIMAL LIFE   The animals that thrive best on Gotska Sandön are the insects. The beetles, in particular, have been the subject of great interest—all 910 species of them. The abundance of pine wood decaying in the sun-warmed sand has made it possible for many species to survive as relicts from earlier, warmer periods. The beetle *Ergates faber,* whose Swedish name means "giant wood buck", can grow to a length of over five centimetres; the island is its most important habitat in Sweden. For at least eight of the beetle species, Gotska Sandön provides the last remaining habitat in Scandinavia.

Due to its isolated location, Gotska Sandön holds a special attraction for migrating birds. Great numbers of smaller birds rest here during the spring and autumn migrations, but only some fifty species remain to hatch and raise their young. The richest bird life is to be found among the broad-leaved woods, where warblers and thrushes are especially numerous. The parrot crossbill and the coal tit are two of the few common species in the pine woods.

Mammals are always poorly represented on islands far from the mainland; on Gotska Sandön, they are limited to the mountain hare and grey seal. Recently, two bat species have been observed as well—the northern and noctule bats.

A well-grown pine forest covers the interior of the island, beautifully decorated with dead trees that have refused to fall. The forest floor is a fragile carpet of heather, mosses, lichens and herbs.

THE HUMAN PRESENCE Today, the island is occupied only by national park personnel. But there was once a resident population of over fifty people—during 1806–1859, when the island was owned by mainland merchants and civil servants. The residents raised crops and cattle, but their principal occupation was logging. Prior to that, the island was owned by the crown and was used for seal-hunting and sheep-herding by the population of Fårö Island.

Logging came to an end in 1950, after which human activity on the island has been limited to maintenance of the park and its buildings. In addition to providing information to park visitors, park personnel use traditional methods to maintain valuable features, including the meadows at Kapellet.

Above: Grey seal pup on the eastern side of Gotska Sandön.
Right: On the southern shore, sandy beaches give way to smooth-polished pebbles and cobbles.
Below: Lesser black-backed gulls gather on the beach to rest.

PETER HANNEBERG

Gotska Sandön – a land of sand

"The light of the sea and the storm-torn, wind-polished pines, bending to the wind further inland, had an otherworldly feel to them, like the open expanses, which thanks to the light seemed vaster than they really were, larger and therefore more palpable, like the solitude, the nearness of the heavens and the sudden stillness."

The wind is northerly. Recalling the poet Bo Setterlind's impressions, recorded fifteen years earlier, I approach Gotska Sandön in a head wind. It is the middle of July, but the sea is no friend today. Getting ashore is fraught with drama. To find shelter, we have to anchor on the roadstead to the south of the island, by Tärnudden point, and are ferried ashore by park rangers in a rubber dinghy. Terra firma at last, after more than two hours on a capricious sea, rolling over the crests of the waves and thudding down into the troughs between them. From Tärnudden, there are eight kilometres of straight-backed pine forest to the lighthouse hamlet at the northern tip of the island.

"There is something sacred and inviolable about this island, affirmed by the timeless, hymnal murmuring in the crowns of its tall pines."

Who would have thought the sea could be so heavy in the middle of the Swedish summer! And yet this was probably just a breeze compared with what winter can hold in store. The notorious Sandön wind, which on many a dark night has driven ships to their doom and which has made this unlikely ridge of sand the Baltic Sea's most legendary scene of shipwreck.

Gotska Sandön is an inaccessible pearl of the Baltic. That is part of its very essence; it *shouldn't* be easy to reach. May it always remain as remote as this, out of the way, shrouded in mystery. It makes a visit more difficult, but also more tempting, and helps to protect this sensitive national park.

Twenty-four hours after our arrival, at Hertas svag on the western shore, as the sun rolls slowly down towards the horizon like a red-hot coal, I lean back among sand dunes which are aglow with the evening light. The light and the landscape take possession of my mind, as yesterday's adventures become a fading dream. This sea, now breathing so gently against the sand, in harmony with the spectacle of the sun's last rays – how could it have been so moody this time yesterday?

The unbroken horizon meets and fuses with the sky. I let light and sand and space become one with my retina, and the feeling of freedom and inaccessibility grows and swells from within. This is something I have only experienced as powerfully in a few other places. On a mountain peak close to the sky, with all earthly things far below me, invisible beneath the clouds. And on a remote sandy island in the Indian Ocean to which I often return, magnificent, unforgettable, a paradise of palms rather than Nordic pines, but without the Nordic light whose sensuality penetrates your body in a way equatorial light never can.

Sandön calls to mind the Skaw peninsula, but one that has been cut off from land, floated off into the Baltic and taken with it the famous light that has inspired Scandinavian artists and poets for over a hundred years. The light, the vastness, the space form the generous setting for my fascination with Sandön.

Beyond the shore and the shifting dunes is the forest, the island's imposing colonnade of soaring pines, rooted only in sand that is held in place by a carpet of mosses, lichens, heather and the roots of grasses and herbs. I leave the path to get closer

Opposite: **Marram and lyme-grass bind the shifting sand at Bredsand.**
Below: **Red helleborine and the white-flowered narrow-leaved helleborine produce a pink hybrid.** Above: **Bird's-eye primrose.**

"From a sea of heather grow pillar-like pines," wrote Albert Engström.
Below: The mountain hare is the only mammal here, apart from the seals.

to what I want to photograph, but deep down it grieves me to step on the dry moss that crunches beneath my feet. I feel that this is somewhere I don't want to tread. I take cautious, carefully calculated steps in the plant cover, which is so thin, so vulnerable, that any wound will be made ever wider by the merciless wind.

Sandön is no dead, solid lump, no monolith of granite or lava fixed unshakably in the earth's crust. This island never rests. It is alive, constantly shifting beneath my feet. The sand dunes, in collusion with the wind, are constantly planning their next move.

But a blanket of plant life and a skin of humus as thin as in a tropical rain forest bind together at least tolerably well what the wind would otherwise sweep away. This covering gives the impression that the older dunes further in from the shore, like Höga åsen—the "High Ridge"—Bourgströms dyn, and the two Slyngdynerna to the north and the south, are unmoving.

Man, the visitor, I myself, must not lay hands or set foot on this intricate and wondrous work, not touch it in any way that could alter or accelerate or harm nature's own plan. On Sandön, this is somehow inherently obvious; you don't need signs or verbal warnings to understand.

No, there is something sacred and inviolable about this island, affirmed by the timeless, hymnal murmuring in the crowns of its tall pines. It would feel quite abhorrent to go lumbering with hobnailed boots into such a sanctuary. Here you feel a reverent respect for what you find, you don't want to cause too many vibrations in a sensitive cathedral, so beautiful and well-built, and yet fragile—built upon the sand.

Gotska Sandön has a will of its own. It is easy to feel an indomitable love for this island, for its self-willed sand dunes which will not be tamed, for its lofty forest that offers a haven from the wind. It is easy to understand the conflicting feelings about the unbridled external forces and the inner harmony of the island which the writer Albert Engström once expressed. Love is so often full of contradictions:

"Imagine a sea of blooming heather. From this sea grow pillar-like pines. And where it thrives best, the heather can grow up to your neck. Or imagine a carpet of moss in all its shifting beauty, spreading as far as the eye can see, with the columns of the trees soaring high into the sky. Imagine deciduous woods interspersed among the pines. Imagine oak woods, birch stands, spinneys of hazel, groves of aspen, thickets of yew, Swedish whitebeam, rowan, goat willow and giant junipers, all protected by pines and the ramparts of the sand-dunes. Even if foul fiends are blowing out at sea or over the island, you can still walk in peaceful stillness down in the valleys, beneath the wildly swaying treetops."

onochamus galloprovincialis is a rare longhorn
eetle that likes the old coniferous forests of
otska Sandön.

egend has it that the crossbill got its twisted
eak trying to pull the nails from the hands and
et of Christ on the cross.

ndön's resident staff live in the lighthouse
mlet near the northern tip of the island. Not
away are a campsite and cabins for visitors.

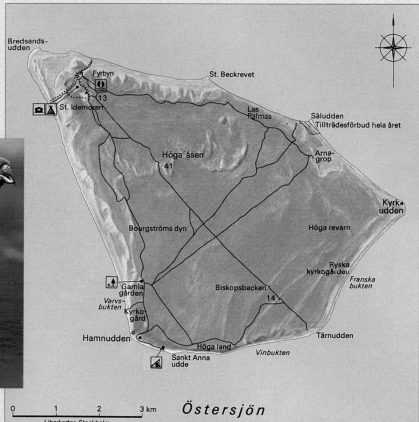

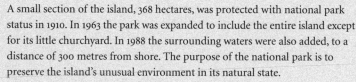

Bredsands-
udden

Fyrbyn
13
St. Idemoren

St. Beckrevet

Las
Palmas

Säludden
Tillträdesförbud hela året

Höga åsen
41

Arna-
grop

Kyrk-
udden

Bourgströms dyn

Höga revarn

Ryska
kyrkogården

Franska
bukten

Gamla
gården

Varvs-
bukten

Kyrko-
gård

Biskopsbacken
14

Hamnudden

Sankt Anna
udde

Höga land

Vinbukten

Tärnudden

0   1   2   3 km
Liberkartor, Stockholm

Östersjön

The "seal lookout pine" sketched by
Albert Engström looks roughly the same
today, over 70 years later.

Foundation	A small section of the island, 368 hectares, was protected with national park status in 1910. In 1963 the park was expanded to include the entire island except for its little churchyard. In 1988 the surrounding waters were also added, to a distance of 300 metres from shore. The purpose of the national park is to preserve the island's unusual environment in its natural state.
Location	In the Baltic Sea, 38 kilometres north of Fårö Island in the Municipality of Gotland, Gotland County.
Area	4490 hectares (11,095 acres), of which 3648 hectares are land surface, including 2913 hectares coniferous forest, six hectares broad-leaved woods, six hectares meadowland, 542 hectares sand dunes, 168 hectares sand beaches and thirteen hectares building sites.
Attractions	The dead trees at Arnagrop. The high ridge. Beetle fauna and bird migrations. The historical buildings and nature centre. The seemingly endless beaches and the sense of isolation.
Visiting Gotska Sandön	There are usually regular boat tours from Fårö Island and the mainland during the summer. The island has no harbour. Visitors may choose to dwell in their own tents, in a large sleeping shelter, or in a cabin. Lodging facilities must be reserved in advance. Visitors who travel to the island with their own boats and wish to spend the night must report to a park official. At the lighthouse compound, the Swedish Environmental Protection Agency has provided a nature centre with an exhibit of the island's natural and human history.

The beetle *Buprestis octoguttata* was
named by Linnaeus. The buprestids are a
family of more than 15,000 species, living
mainly in the tropics. This Swedish species
is associated with pine forests, including
those of Gotska Sandön.

Hamra

At the beginning of the 1900s, Hamra was described as "probably the most remarkable specimen of primeval forest remaining in all of Sweden". Here, undisturbed marshes alternate with ancient, lichen-draped forest in which the trees can be up to 300 years old.

LANDSCAPE Hamra is situated at the junction of Kopparberg, Jämtland and Gävleborg counties, in the sparsely populated region of evergreen forest known as Orsa Finnmark. The area has been greatly affected by waves of logging that twice swept over the landscape. The first, which concentrated on the larger trees, occurred at the start of the 20th century. That was followed years later by the more intensive logging of modern forestry. Hamra is a small remnant of the original forest which has survived unscathed, providing an example of genuine primeval forest.

> "It is a tune like trees soughing in the breeze and whirring dragonflies, yet so muted and soft, as if it were being sung an infinity away."
> KARL-ERIK FORSSLUND (1915)
> (ABOUT THE SIREN OF HAMRA)

The national park is located within a generally flat and marshy landscape that includes scattered patches of low, dry land. Except to the northwest where it borders Lake Svansjön, the national park can be described as a large island of dry land surrounded by open marshes. The gently rolling terrain consists of a few low moraine ridges.

VEGETATION Hamra is Sweden's smallest national park. But in its highly pristine state, it is a small jewel with few parallels outside the mountains along the border with Norway. The odd tree has been felled along the shore of Lake Svansjön, possibly by fishermen; but, otherwise, the trees of the park are completely untouched by axe and saw. The magnificent 300-year-old trees draped in beard-lichen, together with large quantities of dry snags and fallen trunks, form a striking tableau of a genuine primeval forest. Thriving on the decaying trunks are numerous lichens and fungi.

A unique inventory which carefully charted the precise locations of all dead and living trees was carried out in 1922. That was followed up in 1994 by the Swedish University of Agricultural Sciences. A comparison of the two inventories, 72 years apart, confirmed that the dominant pines are gradually being replaced by spruces—a natural development for most moraine forests that are no longer exposed to fire.

Since the early 1700s, the Hamra forest has experienced at least five fires. Such events tend to benefit pine, which is protected from

Hamra is a small remnant of virgin coniferous forest in the south-eastern part of northern Sweden, where the majority of forest land has been commercially exploited.

Näckrostjärnen (above), a pool in the Hamra forest, is fringed by bog mosses, sundews and white beak-sedge (below).

the flames by its thick bark, and which can more easily regenerate itself on burnt ground. Nowadays, in the fire-free and increasingly dense forest, young spruces are better able to establish themselves and eventually force out the pines.

The national park's flora and fauna are typical of small primeval woods on meagre soil. Bilberry, heather, bog bilberry and crowberry dominate the ground cover. A shallow depression in the park's western section has a greater diversity of plants, including wood cranesbill, may lily and the orchids lesser twayblade and creeping lady's tresses. Around the edge of the pond, Näckrostjärn, grow white beak-sedge and the insect-devouring sundew.

ANIMAL LIFE Characteristic bird species include common thrushes and woodpeckers, the willow and other tits, and the Siberian jay. More noteworthy is the insect fauna, especially the wood beetles. The large supply of dead wood is the reason that the park is home to 450 varieties of beetle.

THE HUMAN PRESENCE Hamra is one of the few national parks in Sweden that lacks all trace of human presence, apart from the facilities and visitors resulting from its establishment as a park.

The three-toed woodpecker lives in old-growth forests like Hamra, where there are plenty of hollow trees. Unlike other woodpeckers, it has no red in its plumage.

The common longhorn beetle *Monochamus sutor* gnaws a hollow in the bark of pine or spruce in which to lay its eggs. The larvae bore straight into the wood, where they overwinter.

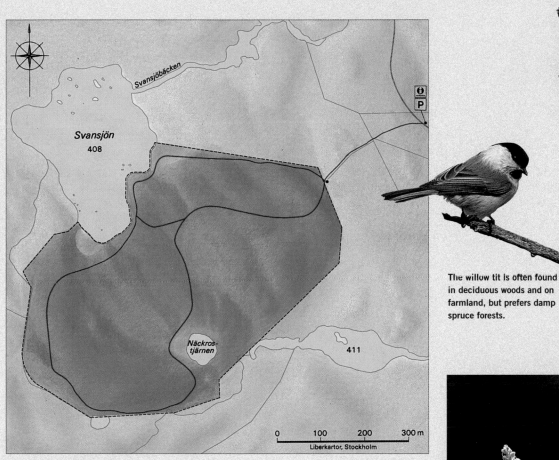

The willow tit is often found in deciduous woods and on farmland, but prefers damp spruce forests.

Foundation	The national park was established in 1909, for the purpose of preserving a section of primeval coniferous forest.
Location	Approximately eight kilometres northeast of Tandsjöborg, and five kilometres east of Highway 81 in the Municipality of Ljusdal, Gävleborg County.
Area	28 hectares (69 acres), of which 21 hectares are coniferous forest and seven hectares marshland, the latter including a small pond.
Attractions	The pristine evergreen forest. The beetle fauna.
Visiting Hamra	The national park can be reached from Highway 81 between Orsa and Sveg, via a turn-off that leads southeast from Lake Fågelsjö. The road passes 300 metres from the park boundary, where there is a parking area and an information display. A trail including sections of boardwalk leads over the marsh and winds through the park.

Creeping lady's tresses grows in moss-carpeted virgin spruce forests like Hamra. The Swedish name for this orchid, "kneeroot", refers to the "knee" at the base of its stem.

Haparanda Skärgård

Haparanda Skärgård National Park in the northernmost waters of the Baltic is an archipelago of sandy islands that has no parallel anywhere else along the coast of Sweden. The low islands bear a resemblance to the atolls of southern seas. Sandskär, with its many dunes, sandy beaches and open, park-like vegetation, is especially appealing.

LANDSCAPE Most of Sweden's archipelagos have a bedrock of gneiss and granite, and are associated with the fissure valley landscape of southern Sweden. But in the Baltic's northern extremity, there is a sizeable archipelago built up entirely of sand and gravel moraine.

Some 2000 years ago, the islands and skerries of today's archipelago were submerged sand banks and moraines. The formation of the islands is the result of post-glacial land elevation, and the transport of gravel and sand by wind and water; both processes still continue today. The land can rise as much as 85 centimetres per century. In the process, coastlines are altered and new islands emerge from the sea at a faster rate than anywhere else in Sweden.

Haparanda Skärgård National Park consists of two larger and some ten smaller islands. It is situated on a flat coastal shelf where the water is seldom deeper than twenty metres. The singular outline of the largest island, Sandskär, is defined by the sand bar that stretches three kilometres in a northerly direction.

Sand and well-formed dunes cover nearly the entire island. Two large, flat, wind-blown areas are surrounded by high dunes and thus resemble public arenas—Östra and Västra Stadion ("East and West Stadiums"). Along the present and former shorelines, there are areas strewn with boulders, large expanses of stone rubble, coastal embankments, and gently curving sand beaches.

The park's other large island, Seskar Furö, is geologically similar to Sandskär; but it is older, thus higher, and more thoroughly

> *"The archipelago between Luleå and Haparanda is like no other. It still has the bright lyricism of the Swedish archipelagos; but at the same time it is swept by an icy blast from the east, bringing with it semi-arctic desolation and Siberian melancholy."*
> STEN SELANDER

The sea around Sandskär is shallow, making landing difficult.

The "West Stadium", with dunes forming a barrier against the sea.

Young deciduous trees near the shore of Sandskär, the largest island.

covered by forest. The other islands are comparatively small; some of them are covered in broad-leaved forest, while others are little more than sand reefs which have only recently emerged from the sea.

VEGETATION Sandskär's vegetation is dominated by heaths that are either completely open or dotted with juniper bushes. Near the middle of the island grows a beautiful mosaic of pine woods and open heath; the trees are short, but have broad trunks and crowns. In the damp hollows, there are groves of aspen and birch. The aspen woods are relatively undisturbed and have the appearance of primeval forest; they have expanded through the sprouting of new trees from the roots of older specimens that grew from seeds.

The forest of Seskar Furö is denser and taller than Sandskär's. In 1982 a storm passed through the area and toppled many of the trees, which were then left undisturbed. Some of the fallen trees are still living, as a result of which the forest has entered an interesting new phase of development.

The plant life of the islands is rather special. In addition to the usual ground shrubs, the dunes and shorelines provide habitat for such interesting species as Bothnian field wormwood, sea pea, sea buckthorn, sea rocket, Nottingham catchfly and the dock *Rumex pseudonatronatus*. The ongoing land elevation is clearly reflected in the vegetation's zonal distribution and the natural succession of species. One example is the expansion of pine forest into previously open areas of heath and sand.

ANIMAL LIFE The islands of the national park are sufficiently large to sustain permanent populations of a few mammals, such as hares and voles. Foxes visit Sandskär every year, and moose are regular visitors to Seskar Furö. Reindeer wander out to the archipelago in the winter, and it happens that the odd reindeer remains behind during the summer. Grey and ringed seals are to be found in the area.

Birds represent the most important feature of the area's animal life. The shallow coastal waters and the islands' strategic location far from the mainland provide ideal conditions for birds pausing on their migration. A total of 230 species have been observed; fifty of them nest in the area. Among the characteristic species are the red-breasted merganser, wryneck, sedge warbler, willow warbler, reed bunting and the park's symbol, the Arctic tern. Also included in the unusually diverse assortment of nesting birds are the pintail, velvet scoter, willow grouse, black grouse, Temminck's stint, turnstone, red-necked phalarope, lesser whitethroat and spotted flycatcher.

THE HUMAN PRESENCE During the Middle Ages, the coastal population began to build harbours, huts and fishing camps at sheltered locations. Since then, land elevation has lifted them higher above the water line. Seal hunting was important well into the 1900s, and a Baltic herring fishery even longer. Some labyrinths, 200-300 years old and laid out with rubblestone, have been found on the islands. A chapel built on Sandskär during the 1760s is still standing today on the south shore of the island, near some clusters of fishing cabins.

Jens Wahlstedt

JENS WAHLSTEDT

Haparanda Sandskär – dunes on an open sea

The shores of Sandskär are still hemmed in by great belts of drift-ice as we round the southern tip of the island and head in towards the fishing village of Kumpula. And yet it is the second week in June, with a scorching summer sun shining down on the Bothnian Bay. On the far horizon, towards Malören and the sea, we can see unbroken lines of white seal ice, drifting where the wind chooses to send it.

Staffan Svanberg from Haparanda reduces speed and edges the MS *Bosmina* carefully in between the ice-floes. We are witnessing a time of upheaval, typical of the regions around the Arctic Circle. In just a few days' time, all the ice will have gone. The constant daylight and the penetrating warmth of the sun consume it at record speed. Seabirds already crowd the patches of open water, and trees are in leaf around the chapel and the wind-bleached timber buildings of Kumpula.

Sandskär is far out at sea, a good thirty kilometres from the mainland. Its cottages and outhouses recall the fishing culture of centuries past, when boats made their way here from the Finnish and Swedish coasts in search of herring. Nowadays, though, for all but a few brief weeks in summer, Sandskär is a desert island. The descendants of the fishermen use the old huts as summer cottages, and the occasional ornithologist will brave the treacherous spring ice or autumn gales to come out here.

We disembark at the old stone pier, and are met by a devout silence. A tang of salt and melting sea ice fills the air, last year's grass sighs in the wind, and meadow pipits sing above the sandy heath. We are soon installed in one of the cottages, with a crackling fire in the hearth. Coffee and a warm fireside are just the thing after the long sea crossing from Seskarö.

In the evening we follow the narrow path of stepping-stones across the heath from the fishing village to the chapel. Everywhere we see memorials to the island's fishing heyday. Small mounds of stones arranged in regular rows, once supports for the racks on which the fishermen dried their nets. Here and there, large salt pits in the sand. Old navigation marks broken off by storms and now far from the shore.

They are all tell-tale signs of what went on on Haparanda Sandskär at the beginning of the century. Fishing crews from places such as Nikkala and Seskarö spent entire summers here catching herring. The spring seal hunt was another important livelihood. Up to 1915, around twenty crews could be found on the island, with two to three men in each. Women and children came along too, and they brought goats with them to provide milk. Sandskär offered the island equivalent of the summer pastures of the mountains, and traces of the paddocks where the animals grazed can still be seen around Kumpula.

The fishermen's chapel enthroned in the middle of the island is presumably one of the simplest edifices belonging to the Church of Sweden. It is said to have begun life as a parish granary, outside Björkö Church in Finland, from which grain was distributed to those in need during years of famine. In 1809 the chapel was sold to the Swedes, and soon after that it was provided with a bell, cast in Stockholm.

The bleached red timber of the chapel fits in well with the

"Sand is the basis for everything here. The entire island is the product of a dynamic creative act."

Below: The Haparanda archipelago rises only slightly above the horizon. Above: Cowberries (lingonberries).

"The birchwoods remind us of the mountains. We start suddenly at the alarm call of a willow grouse."

threefold desolation of its setting – heath, sky and sea. The interior, too, has a distinctive solemnity. Everything is spartan and rough-hewn, from the simple beams of shipwreck timber that serve as pews to the white-painted communion rail and the herring barrel with its birch besom.

From the roof, we can see the four well-preserved stepping-stone paths leading to the chapel across the sandy heath. They were built to allow those wanting to get to it to ring the bell or attend a service to do so without getting sand in their shoes. Fishermen from Tornio in Finland are known to have come out to Sandskär back in the late eighteenth century, which was when the chapel was moved here. The different boat crews took it in turns to ring the bell, either to summon the faithful to prayer, to announce the departure of the fishing boats, or to warn of fog.

Early the next morning we head across the heath to Östviken, and on our way pass a remarkable number of different habitat types for such a small area, so far out at sea. Birch groves of the kind you find in the mountains, wetlands and lagoons, virgin forests of aspen, pinewoods, gently sloping beaches that make excellent resting grounds for waders and seabirds.

Sand is the basis for everything here. The entire island is the product of a dynamic creative act, in which sand from the sea-bed was swept up by the wind and gradually bound together by lyme-grass, stunted bird cherry and carpets of crowberry. The tallest of the dunes rises to a height of twenty metres.

The birchwoods remind us of the mountains. We start suddenly at the alarm call of a willow grouse, and stumble on rein-deer bones. And in the bushes we hear the singing of a blue-throat or ring ouzel, or a rustic bunting. But we also come across species from the far south, like the golden oriole and

bee-eater. It is these contrasts which make Sandskär so exotic. The island's position in the sea is like a magnet to migrating birds. Eastern species from Russia, such as Indian tree pipit and yellow-browed warbler, make the combination unbeatable.

In Östviken the net traps are being checked prior to the morning's bird ringing session. Since many years, volunteers from the Norrbotten Ornithological Society have been running the ornithological observatory on Haparanda Sandskär on a systematic basis. I remember when we created the embryo of it far back in the early 1960s.

Down the years, more than 60,000 birds, representing 118 species, have been ringed on Sandskär, and roughly one per cent of them have been recovered in other parts of the world. Breeding bird surveys and counts of migrating birds are also carried out here. So far, 231 bird species have been observed on the island, something of a record for such a northerly site.

There is much to interest the botanist, too, on Haparanda Sandskär. The best months are July and August, when even down by the boathouses you are met by a bright display of red rosebay willowherb and autumn-yellow tansy. At night, Nottingham catchfly opens its petals and dispenses its powerful, hyacinth-like fragrance. A Bothnian subspecies of field worm-wood (*Artemisia campestris* ssp. *bottnica*) is another speciality, confined to the islands along the coast of northern Sweden. The hair-grass *Deschampsia bottnica* is not found anywhere in the world outside the Bothnian Bay.

Back by the fishermen's cottages, the sea is sparkling like a mirror between the boathouses. The drift-ice has shrunk to mere fragments, and through binoculars we can see the fast ice off Malören moving out into the Bay. The radio promises northerly winds, which means we won't have any trouble with drift-ice.

Out here on this lonely island, so far from land, the shipping forecasts are all important. Before the harbour channel was dredged a few years ago, it was impossible to land or leave here in anything stronger than a fresh breeze. I remember being storm-bound out here with my family once in the 1960s. Our provisions ran low, and we survived for a whole week on smoked whitefish and crispbread. Haparanda Sandskär is a real outpost.

In recent years, more and more people have discovered and been fascinated by the remarkable natural features and cultural history of Sandskär. And it is gratifying that the island is now fully protected. First, in 1960, it was declared a nature reserve and then, in 1995, it became part of the Haparanda Archipelago National Park.

"Sandskär has a virgin, arctic beauty all its own; and in my mind's eye it is already tossing, half-unreal, on the summer sea of a Nordic odyssey," was how, in the 1950s, the writer-botanist Sten Selander described the then little known island.

Every time I leave Haparanda Sandskär I watch through binoculars as the chapel and the fishermen's cottages gradually disappear below the horizon. Undisturbed by civilization and the ravages of time. A slumbering Ithaca. An island of birds, and of contrasts.

And always I long to return.

Thanks to a good supply of voles and hares, the red fox has remained in residence.

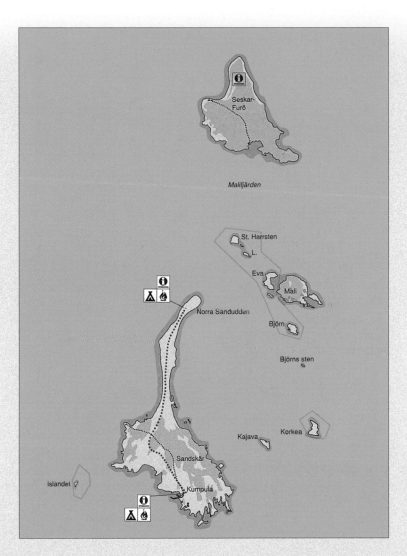

Artemisia campestris ssp. *bottnica*, a local Bothnian subspecies of field wormwood, grows on Sandskär.

The Arctic tern, symbol of the Haparanda Skärgård National Park, nests here in large numbers.

Foundation	Haparanda Archipelago National Park was established in 1995, for the purpose of preserving a unique archipelago landscape in an essentially natural state.
Location	Near the border with Finland in the northernmost section of the Baltic Sea, in the Municipality of Haparanda, Norrbotten County.
Area	6000 hectares (14,826 acres). 770 hectares are dry land, of which 170 hectares are evergreen forest, 132 hectares broad-leaved forest, 262 hectares heath, 92 hectares meadowland and 114 hectares sandy clearings with boulders. The largest island is Sandskär, with some 400 hectares.
Attractions	Nordrevet, Västra Stadion and the chapel on Sandskär. The sandy beaches and dunes. The migrating birds.
Visiting Haparanda Skärgård	It is difficult to land on the islands of the archipelago, due to the shallow water. One of the few safe landing sites for larger boats is on Sandskär's northern sandbar, Nordrevet. From there, a trail leads to the fishing camp of Kumpula, where there are sleeping cabins, tentsites, a sauna and an information display. For the protection of nesting birds, landing on some of the smaller islands around Sandskär is prohibited from May 1 to July 31 every year.

A reindeer on a summer visit to the island passes the curious chapel. It found its way here in the winter, across the ice.

The Swedish name for the ringed seal, *vikare* ('bay seal') refers to the bays and sounds where it is often found. In winter it can be seen on ice floes out at sea.

Muddus

A section of the Swedish taiga has been preserved in Muddus National Park , where it is possible to experience undisturbed primeval forest, raging waterfalls, the solitude of broad marshes, and an animal life that is typical for what remains of Norrland's unspoiled nature.

LANDSCAPE The inland of upper Norrland is a large flatland of low-lying forests and marshes, dotted with a few isolated conical hills. The technical term for such a landscape is "monadnock plain"; it is widespread in Sweden and Finland, but found nowhere else in Europe. The conical hills are remnants of harder bedrock which has resisted erosion better than that of surrounding areas.

Muddus is representative of upper Norrland's monadnock plain, with marshes, forests, and hills that can reach up to 200 metres above the surrounding flatland. Low ridges run from the western moun-tains into the complex of marshes in the centre of the park. The bedrock slopes gently through the park toward the Stora Lule River, where it plunges 200 metres into the valley. This is the site of the park terrain's only dramatic feature—a series of deep canyons.

Almost the entire park is drained to the south by the Muddusjokk River, which abruptly plunges 42 metres over the raging Muddus Falls before continuing southward through a deep canyon. Below the falls lies a perfectly round small lake. The terrain along the canyon is wild and rugged, with nearly vertical walls up to 100 metres high. Enormous boulders are still being pried loose by the expansion of ice, to tumble into the river or accumulate along its narrow bank.

VEGETATION The forest is dominated in the central and western sections of the park by spruce, and in the south and west by pine. There are also mixed forests of spruce, pine and birch in many places.

Opposite: Vast, waterlogged mires are typical of the central part of Muddus.
Below: A great grey owl on an undisturbed blanket of snow, perhaps with prey in its talons. This is a species associated above all with Norrbotten.

The vegetation on some of the hills that rise above the tree line has much the character of alpine heath.

The marshes of Muddus are comparatively shallow, and incorporate many small islands of dry land. Over half the total marsh area comprises a sort of gridwork formed by alternating patches of solid and wet ground; such areas are very difficult to traverse. The large flat marshland in the centre of the park includes a number of lakes and streams. Along the edges of the marshes and lakes are wetland woods that contribute to the park's biological diversity.

The character of the original taiga landscape has in many places been fundamentally altered by roads and logging, but it can still be experienced in Muddus National Park. One reason that the area has escaped logging is that the main watercourse, the Muddusjokk River, is not suitable for rafting timber. The park's oldest living pine has attained an age of 720 years. Research indicates that at least 47 summer forest fires have occurred during the period from 1413-1946. The magnificent primeval forest, with its broad-beamed trees, charred stumps and snags, contributes greatly to the national park's wilderness character.

Growing in the marshes of Muddus are such common plants as

The bottom step of the 42 metre high Muddusfallet waterfall, in a particularly wild part of the national park.

Viewed against the light, the parasols of the moss *Splachnum luteum* seem almost fluorescent.

the bottle and slender sedges, cloudberry and bog bilberry. Among the more unusual species are alpine bartsia, whortle-leaved willow, alpine meadow rue and yellow marsh saxifrage. On the rock walls of the Muddusjokk River canyon there is an interesting flora that includes *Antennaria alpina*, alpine catchfly and the related *Silene furcata*.

ANIMAL LIFE   Larger predators are represented in Muddus by a permanent bear population, along with a handful of lynxes and wolverines. Moose (elk), pine martens and weasels are more com-mon, and otters may also be spotted along the many streams.

There are many varieties of birds, especially wading and water birds. The park's most characteristic species is the whooper swan, which nests among the central marshes. The goldeneye is typically seen on the lakes, the wood sandpiper and crane in the marshes. Less frequent species include the smew, bean goose, broad-billed sand-piper and jacksnipe.

Often-sighted birds of prey include the osprey and the hen harrier; the golden eagle is also a regular visitor. The Tengmalm's and Ural owls, and the capercaillie and hazelhen, all live in these

coniferous forests. All told, 115 bird species have been sighted in the park, and about fifty of them nest here.

THE HUMAN PRESENCE   Muddus is used for reindeer grazing by several Saami villages. Despite the area's difficult access, some mid-18th century settlers established themselves near Lake Muddusjaure, where they lived for over fifty years before abandoning the site in 1909. Scientific research in the area was begun in 1926. Muddus is one of the most well-researched and documented areas of coniferous forest in the country.

Top: **Spruce forest in Muddus, dressed for the winter.**
Left: **The mountain hare changes colour according to the season, and when motionless it becomes almost part of the snow cover.**

An ant-hill in the park's coniferous forest.

Porjus

A Ural owl on its nest stump.

The remote mires and lakes of Muddus make are ideal for the whooper swan.

Muddus National Park has a population of brown bears.

Foundation The national park was established in 1942, for the purpose of preserving a mixed marsh-forest landscape in its natural state. In 1967, Muddus National Park was awarded the European Council's Diploma for Nature Conservation. Muddus is also included in the 940,000 hectares of the Laponian Area, which in 1996 was designated by UNESCO as a World Heritage Site.

Location South of the highway between Porjus and Gällivare, in the municipalities of Gällivare and Jokkmokk, Norrbotten County.

Area 50,350 hectares (124,415 acres). 48,900 hectares are land area, of which 21,000 hectares are marshland, 27,670 hectares forest, 50 hectares open heath, and 180 hectares boulders and rock outcrops.

Attractions The primeval forest, especially the giant pine. The great mosaic of marsh and forest. The deep canyons. Muddus Falls. The bird life.

Visiting Muddus The easiest way to reach the park is by road from Liggadammen. From the road's terminus at Skaite, there is a hiking trail to Muddus Falls and Måskokårså. The paths from Solaure and Sarkavare also connect with the park's trail system. There are four sleeping cabins and two simpler tourist huts along the trails. A bird observation tower at Muddusluobbal offers a view over the marshes. In order to protect nesting birds in the areas around Lake Muddusjaure, Sörstubba and Måskokårså River, access is prohibited from March 15 to July 31 every year.

Norra Kvill

Norra Kvill is a genuine primeval forest in the region of Småland. Hardly anywhere else in southern Sweden is it possible to experience such a pristine evergreen forest. The national park offers a fascinating stroll through a landscape of moss-covered boulders and enchanted lakes, and up to an exquisite view from the summit of the highest hill.

LANDSCAPE   Norra Kvill is situated in the northeastern corner of Småland. The national park's terrain is gently rolling, with a maximum height of sixty metres from hillcrest to valley floor. The hill called Idhöjden has a distinctive crown that peaks at 230 metres above sea level. The remainder of the park consists of lower hills and the hollows between them. Boulders are strewn about the moraine soils which cover much of the area. In some places, especially at the feet of steep slopes, large heaps of boulders have accumulated. The bedrock of Småland granite lies exposed at several locations.

Left: Uprooted trees, straight pines and moss-carpeted ground are the trademarks of Norra Kvill.
Below: A typical forest bird found in the national park is the hazelhen. The burring sound of its flight has earned it the epithet "the bird that makes a lot of noise".

Moss-covered boulders and windthrown pines that have already started to decay.

VEGETATION Evergreen forest covers nearly the entire surface of the national park. In addition to mixed coniferous forest dominated by pines, there are lesser stands of spruce with abundant flowering plants, as well as sections of wetland spruce. The flower-carpeted spruce woods grow on slopes that are rich in nutrients, as well as in brook ravines where some of the trees are as tall as 35 metres. It is here that the greatest floral diversity is to be found. In the park's south-eastern section is an especially fertile ravine with such broad-leaved trees as elm, ash, oak and lime, along with smaller species such as bird cherry, hazel and guelder rose.

In the centre of the park lies Stora Idgölen, a small lake with water lilies; it also goes under the name of Trolltjärnen. The lake lies in the heart of the national park, surrounded by small marshes and beautiful pristine forest that has not been logged for the past 150 years. Due to the steep and rocky terrain, farming has always been impossible, and logging difficult. The ancient pines and the many decaying trees create a bewitching atmosphere of primeval forest. Many of the pines are over 350 years old.

The national park has an unusually diverse flora for an evergreen forest. All of 200 mosses, 100 lichens and 200 higher plant species have been identified. In the drier spruce woods grow hepatica, spring pea, bush vetch and early dog violet. In the wetland forest near one of the small lakes grow bog arum, marsh violet and tufted loosestrife. Spring pasque-flower and yellow birdsnest can be found in the sparse pine woods on higher ground. Among the area's most exclusive species is wood fescue, for which the national park is the only known site in Småland.

ANIMAL LIFE The mammals of Norra Kvill include the moose, roe deer, mountain hare, fox, badger, pine marten and red squirrel. There are also several species of bats, which dwell in the hollow trees. The bird life of the park is exceptionally diverse. The undisturbed forest, with its numerous dead and dying trees, provides excellent opportunities for birds to find food and nesting sites. Species that nest in the park include the capercaillie, black grouse, hazelhen, crested tit, coal tit, treecreeper and pygmy owl.

THE HUMAN PRESENCE The forests of Småland have previously been inhabited and exploited to a far greater degree than one might imagine. But the primeval forest in the central section of Norra Kvill National Park is a notable exception. As far as is known, no humans have ever dwelt here. The only building is a small field-shed by a marsh near the park's eastern boundary. The oldest survey map of the area was drawn in 1836, at which time the area was described as, "woodland on rocky ground, with both healthy and dry old pine trees that are difficult to fetch due to the area's difficult terrain". Thus the forest was considered to be unsuitable for logging.

GERDA ANTTI

Norra Kvill – an enchanted forest

A path wide enough for two to walk easily side by side leads to the Norra Kvill National Park.

On the way there, you pass meadows, fields and pastures, all solidly and arduously enclosed by stone walls, as tall as they are wide. Some of the territories they once defended are no longer intact, invaded by spruces and birches, and often plump lilac bushes as well, as local farmers have faded out of the picture. One thing that becomes patently clear as you head towards your destination is that rocks are something people here were never short of. Millions of them have been prized from the ground and dragged away and laid side by side and one on top of the other. Taken from the fields to make way for grain, and from the pastures to make room for livestock.

And the path to Norra Kvill is itself testimony to the fact that the farmers did not have to look very far for their raw materials, consisting as it does of equal quantities of stones, roots and soil. It is not a good idea to gaze up at the tall pines around you for more than a few moments at a time as you walk along.

"This is the sort of place where we Swedes feel reverence and respect for our forests. We have forests in our blood."

Begin by looking at the path itself, with its coarse roots and stones, reminiscent of the back of the hand of someone old and wise, crisscrossed with veins and sinews. Then look up at the pines to your right. So tall, and so slender. Yet you would need very long arms to reach right round them, and few people have arms that long. At their feet are springy cushions of bilberry and cowberry, now, in the early summer, the tenderest of yellow-greens, and the cowberry plants are in flower. Follow the trunks with your gaze, lifting your eyes ever higher. If you want to play safe, stand still and keep a steadying hand on the back of your neck.

For the first eighteen metres or so, there is not a branch to be seen. And as you behold the trunks and their bark, you realize how cruel and unjust a fate befalls all those pine trees that are felled before they attain their greatest beauty. A pine of seventy-five summers has a bark that can compare in pattern and character with a leopard skin. These pines are the panthers of the forest, fortunately the only ones and the most beautiful. A soaring pine forest always gives me a sense of freedom. A feel-

ing – fleeting maybe, but there all the same – of the happy and uplifting potential inherent in everything.

The wanderers who pass this way ten, twenty years from now, will they stumble across the same massive obstacle as I do today – a spruce that has reached its final resting place? A tall, jagged stump, split down to the roots? Was lightning its executioner?

Chickweed wintergreen and may lily are in flower, and spindle-tree. The ferns are making rapid progress, well on their way to growing as tall and tropical-looking as only they can in a Swedish forest. Coarse, broad planks, carefully made to measure, provide a walkway over the boggier spots. By one of them,

Above: **Bog arum, a splash of colour in a dark forest fen.**
Below: **"This is a shore where only fairies can dance,"**
writes Gerda Antti, referring to Lake Idgölen.

Twinflower "watches through the light summer nights and is at its most fragrant then," the botanist C. F. Nyman wrote in 1867.

a frog leaps in alarm, beautiful and a warm reddish-brown. A squirrel, in the full red of its summer coat, scampers along a log, then stops in its tracks and looks round, its tail quivering.

The path starts to climb, and you now feel you are entering virgin forest proper. Moss, thick and green, covers the boulders that are piled up between the tall spruces with their drooping, trailing branches. However big they are, these rocks look like soft cushions in their velvet wrappings. An epidemic of bark beetles has struck, leaving a trail of disease and death, and trees still reeling from the effects are tilted in all directions over the ones that have already succumbed. Chunks of pine bark, thick and densely layered like tomes of seven hundred pages, litter the ground around the trunk they once clothed, which is now as smooth as a bald pate. One lesson the forest teaches you is that losing your bark is a greater calamity than losing your hair.

After a short uphill stretch, the footpath comes out at Stora Idgölen, despite its name a lake of only modest proportions. Between the water lilies, its surface is still and smooth. There are no fish keeping watch, only pond skaters going quietly about their business. The pleasant, slightly pungent fragrance of Labrador tea hangs in the air. What a pretty flower crowns its narrow, green-brown leaves! And the sight of cloudberries in bloom is enough to make anyone's mouth water.

The ground near the water's edge gives beneath my feet, and water wells up around my boots. If the Nix lives anywhere, it certainly isn't in clear, shallow streams, as most people seem to believe; it can only be here. So I go no further out, and step back onto firmer ground. This is a shore where only fairies can dance.

And who knows what happens in the forest by night? Even by moonlight I wouldn't venture out to discover the answer. Little wonder there were so many trolls in the days before human beings discovered the profits to be made from forests.

I saw a sign once in a shop selling books of fairy tales: "So you don't believe in trolls? Then go into the forest alone one night..."

The path goes on. To me, a forest path is something alluring, a siren of the woods. Isn't it leading in the wrong direction now? Wasn't that last signpost a bit unclear? There is nothing for it but to follow the path wherever it leads. Wherever it goes, here the path is your only refuge and guide.

The footpath twists and turns like a brook, its curves always smooth. Sometimes wider and sometimes narrower, it forges on, further and further into the forest. Why go straight if you can avoid it? Straight lines are unnatural, a human invention.

Here there are spruces and pines that have died at their posts, that haven't even fallen. Half-grown, once green spruces are now silvery-grey skeletons. If there are no fairies dancing here, the mosquitoes certainly are. Not as big as their northern Swedish cousins, but with the sort of persistence you would expect in Småland.

The high spot of the forest, literally, is Idhöjden, where there is nothing to obstruct your line of vision. A green Sweden opens up, just forest and a glistening lake. After shuddering at the sight of the sheer drop below, I sit here for a while. This is the sort of place where we Swedes feel reverence and respect for our forests. We have forests in our blood.

On the way down, the darkness of moss and spruce returns, the wild and dramatic scenes of huge trees that have tumbled head-first down the slopes and come to rest one on top of the other. It is so silent, the crashing of timber has long since died away, and everything is now swathed in moss. What is concealed beneath it? What will take your weight, and what will not?

This is how it was a long time ago, before we human beings imposed straight lines on everything. Even in the forests, we now build roads and plant trees in regimented rows. Virgin forest is neither young nor old, it is eternal, it comes and goes. We ourselves may live to be a hundred at best, but here there are pine trees more than 350 years old. And not far from Norra Kvill is the Rumskulla Oak, which, at the grand old age of nine hundred, can call most other things small fry.

When you have left the park, treat yourself to a few hours exploring the capriciously signposted minor roads around here. You will always arrive somewhere, some time. Drive as if you were following a footpath in the forest, hold on for a while to the natural mood in which you have just been immersed. Journey on empty roads of crunching gravel or silent asphalt, through seemingly never-ending forests, whose trees are mere infants compared with the giants you have just seen. Past scattered red-painted houses that spring out from a lush, leafy green. Cranes grazing in a field, an elk knee-deep in water, watch as you drive slowly by.

Treat yourself to a gradual return to contemporary living. Keep the song of the forest within you as long as you can.

Yellow birdsnest is a remarkable, fleshy plant, with scales rather than leaves, an indirect parasite that lives in association with mycorrhizal fungi in the soil, which in turn live on pine roots.

Grey and dishevelled, the omnivorous badger emerges from its set at dusk.

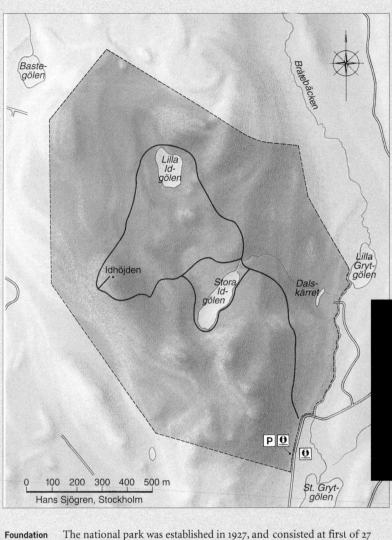

Hans Sjögren, Stockholm

The crested tit can be found in the forests of Norra Kvill and on the surrounding farmland until late in the year.

Daubenton's bat is common throughout Sweden. In forests, it lives in colonies in hollow trees and flies over lakes at night hunting for large insects.

Rhagium inquisitor is a common longhorn beetle. Its larvae pupate under the bark of the dead conifers found in Norra Kvill.

Foundation	The national park was established in 1927, and consisted at first of 27 hectares. Later, a buffer zone of approximately the same size was given the status of crown reserve. Following the acquisition of additional land, the park was expanded in 1984 to its present size of 111 hectares.
Location	Roughly ten kilometres north of Rumskulla in the Municipality of Vimmerby, Kalmar County.
Area	111 hectares (274 acres) of which two hectares are water surface. The land area consists of 104 hectares evergreen forest, one hectare mixed forest and four hectares marshland.
Attractions	The primeval forest, and the wild terrain with its huge boulders. The enchanted lakes of the forest. The view from Idhöjden.
Visiting Norra Kvill	The national park is located near the road between Vimmerby and Norra Vi, seven kilometres south of Ydrefors. A signed turn-off leads to a parking area, where there is an information display on the area's natural history. An occasionally steep hiking trail leads past the two lakes, and up to an excellent outlook on Idhöjden.

Padjelanta

Padjelanta is set in a mountain region of high plains and majestic lakes. The soft contours of the open landscape contrast sharply with the dramatic profile of the nearby Sarek Mountains. The national park includes some of the most luxuriant flowering meadows in the Swedish mountains, as well as most of the bird species associated with the heaths and lakes of the barren heights.

LANDSCAPE The Saami name, Padjelanta, means "the higher land", which certainly applies to this plain some 700 metres above sea level. It is an area of broad alpine heaths and level depressions set amidst the swelling crests and ridges of the mountains. With their broad expanses of water and surrounding treeless plain, lakes Virihaure and Vastenjaure possess a very special beauty.

The southern section of the park is dominated by a crescent of high massifs. The highest among them, Jeknaffo, is over 1800 metres above sea level and offers a magnificent view that reaches all the way to the Lofoten Islands off the coast of Norway.

Padjelanta's bedrock consists for the most part of rocks that are easily eroded and rich in lime, which is reflected in the luxuriant

Left: Dust swirls in the sunset as herders of the Sirkas district mark their reindeer calves in the corral. Below: Arctic fox with this year's cubs.

In 1948, after a trek along the lakes of Padjelanta, author and botanist Sten Selander wrote: "Virihaure is not only perhaps the most beautiful of Sweden's mountain lakes, but also the brightest and most cheerful."

alpine vegetation. A remarkable geological feature of the park is the ultra-basic serpentine rock, known for its high concentration of heavy metals. Another interesting feature is the area of flat "Kisuris Terraces" in the northeast section, which formed in the delta of a meltwater lake when the last ice age glacier retreated through the area some 7000 years ago. Southeast of Staluluokta is one of the mountains' largest complexes of tundra polygons, which are formed when heavy frost forces up patches of ground in ring-like patterns.

Padjelanta is located 300 kilometres from the Atlantic Ocean, which contributes to the area's heavy precipitation. In the mountains along the border with Norway, patches of snow may remain until mid-July. On the border mountain, Sierkatjåkkå, is one of Sweden's largest glaciers.

VEGETATION Nearly the entire national park is located above the tree line. The only wooded areas are a few small stands of mountain birch in the northeast section of the park. Padjelanta is well-known as one of the richest flower sites in the Swedish mountains, with over 400 vascular plants. On the meadows and slopes south of Lake Virihaure grow such hungry species as mountain avens, alpine arnica, Arctic woodrush, Arctic rhododendron (Lapland rosebay), alpine whitlow-grass, flame-coloured lousewort, Arctic harebell and northern catchfly. Aralåbtå, which rises from Lake Vastenjaure's north shore, is a steep incline with high flowery meadows, heaths and thickets of willow. It is also the site of such rarities as the primrose *Primula stricta*, dark red helleborine and

"When I came up into it, I did not know whether I was in Asia or Africa, for the soil, the situation and all the herbs were unknown to me. I had now arrived in the mountains."
CAROLUS LINNAEUS (1732)

whorled Solomon's seal. Due to the calcium-rich soils, heaths cover much of the high plains, and thus contribute to its open nature.

The heavy metals in the ultra-basic serpentine rock produce a toxic effect that only extremely hardy plants can survive. The most remarkable of these is probably the sandwort *Arenaria humifusa*, the nearest alternative sites of which are located on Spitzbergen and Greenland.

ANIMAL LIFE Of the resident mammals, the wolverine and Arctic fox are of particular interest. Otherwise, the mammals of Padjelanta are limited in number and variety. But most of the birds associated with Sweden's barren mountains and alpine lakes are represented in the park. Characteristic species of the open heaths include the golden plover, meadow pipit and wheatear; the ptarmigan, dotterel and whimbrel are also present. In areas of willow and smaller lakes, there are often many ducks, for example the long-tailed duck, teal and common scoter, as well as wading birds such as the ruff, red-necked (northern) phalarope, Temminck's stint and redshank. Common smaller birds in the willow and birch woods are the redpoll, willow warbler, Lapland bunting (longspur), bluethroat and redwing.

The rough-legged buzzard and long-tailed skua are fairly common during good lemming years, when even the seldom-seen snowy owl may nest in the area. Other interesting species are the lesser white-fronted goose, golden and white-tailed eagles and gyrfalcon.

THE HUMAN PRESENCE Padjelanta has attracted humans for centuries. Traces include Stone Age pitfalls for trapping reindeer. The park is used for fishing and summer grazing by the Saami villages of Sirka, Jåkkåkaska and Tuorpon. It holds great interest for natural scientists, and is highly valued among mountain tourists.

Anders Bjärvall

ANDERS BJÄRVALL

A Padjelanta diary

Marking reindeer calves is a waiting game. Waiting for the right weather. Waiting until the reindeer can be driven into the corral.

And so it was on 4 July 1984. I was camped up at Arasluokta, waiting in the wet with herders from the Jåkkåkaska reindeer husbandry district. It was no more than four degrees above freezing when we awoke, and not much warmer later in the day. A steady drizzle descended, clouds hung low over the ground, and the hours rolled slowly by.

Certainly it was an exciting project that had brought me up here. The nature conservation authorities and the Sami have always had differing views on the impact of predatory animals on reindeer. Now, together, we were going to attach radio transmitters to reindeer calves, and later use them to track down any that were killed.

"The rain had finally stopped and it was a beautiful night – light, still and cool."

Ibba and Amul Läntha plied me with bread freshly baked in the hot embers, as we reclined on reindeer skins in their traditional herding tent, waiting and talking about wild animals. Amul, the elder of the district, was over 80 then and had a lot to tell.

When we grew tired of waiting, we made ourselves go out into the wet, but light, night. In the birchwoods on the slopes of Aras, a garden warbler sang through the rain to proclaim that it was summer after all. We wandered in the direction of Allak. The flat landscape around us, with its many small lakes, was once the haunt of the lesser white-fronted goose. Now only velvet scoters and long-tailed ducks were to be seen on the water, while the odd redshank flew in anxious warning above our heads.

Padjelanta is also the land of the Arctic fox, so when, around midnight, we suddenly came across a fox, we assumed it to be the Arctic species. But it turned out to be a red fox with very unusual markings, light and blotchy, with a bushy, gleaming yellow-white tail.

On our return to Arasluokta on the Friday evening, the first herdsman we met informed us that, despite the rain, the reindeer had already started to be driven from the east and that the plan was to start work at midnight. By just after five the following morning, we were soaked to the skin, but we had equipped fifty two-month-old reindeer calves with transmitters. In due course, they would provide us with unique information about reindeer mortality and its causes.

I had often heard that the Sami didn't work with their reindeer on Sundays. But suddenly it was decided that a new enclosure to capture the animals was to be built on a pasture along the Mielätno river. At eight in the morning, now into the fifth day of almost incessant rain, we gathered there, and eight hours later had created a corral of more than a hectare, with long arms

Opposite: **The view from Jeknaffo (1,836 m) is panoramic; here, looking north.** Below: **Padjelanta is used by three reindeer husbandry districts.** Above: **Mountain avens.**

The Sami of Sirkas live in traditional tents in Padjelanta during the summer calf-marking season. Skuolla on the boundary with Sarek.

stretching up towards Huornatj to guide the reindeer in.

On Sunday night we sat on a hill some distance away and watched the herd approach. The rain had finally stopped and it was a beautiful night – light, still and cool. A solitary Lapland bunting sang from the top of a willow bush.

From a distance, a herd of reindeer looks like a huge, dynamic amoeba. One moment it is long and narrow, the next it is compressed to become short and wide. Small protrusions grow in different directions, only to be driven back by the herdsmen and their dogs. When the over 2,000-strong herd flowed smoothly into the corral, even we visitors felt a great sense of satisfaction. And we felt even better eleven hours later, when we had kitted out another 130 calves with collars and transmitters.

On 20 May 1985 I was in Stockholm working most of the day. As I cycled home, a thrush nightingale was singing and girls were soaking up the sun in the park. A few hours later I landed in Gällivare – in squally snow showers, and just one degree above freezing! Sometimes Sweden feels long, especially when one season is handing over to the next.

It was spring in Padjelanta, too, but not the sort of spring that encouraged sunbathing. To read off the reindeer collars through binoculars on the southern and eastern slopes of Arasluokta, we had to crouch behind boulders to shelter from the icy blast.

But there were plenty of both cows and calves to be seen. Around them, three white-tailed eagles were on patrol, with an eager entourage of hooded crows, ravens and gulls. Where the ground was clear of snow, golden plovers and snow buntings were resting.

The stiff easterly wind proved useful a few days later, when we were able to go down to the shore of Lake Virihaure, stand on our skis on the ice and be swept along like ice-yachts. An odd experience for the end of May.

Over the next six days, we zigzagged along the northern flank of Tuipenjarka, over the pass between Allak and Mattåive, eastwards along the banks of the Mielätno and finally along the eastern slope of Alatjåkkå, down to Lake Alkajaure. Now skiing, now walking, and finding one small herd of reindeer after another, with countless collars recorded as a result.

Some females had already lost their young. It was interesting to find that they hadn't all been killed by predators. At Mattåive, we caught sight of a dead calf which, from a distance, looked as if it had attracted the attention of numerous beasts of prey. But when we got to it, it turned out that all the tracks had been made by the mother. She was grazing a short distance away and had kept returning to her dead offspring, which was lying on the snow with no outward signs of injury.

One evening a year later, in May 1986, we met the herdsmen of the Jåkkåkaska district down in Jokkmokk. Our field work was nearing completion and we were discussing and assessing the results. Amul, now 82, was also there.

Late that evening, when our meeting came to an end, he took me aside to talk. I could still picture him hard at work all night in the corral, with all the energy of a young man. But it wasn't the results of the study he was wanting to discuss.

Amul, the district elder, was proud that reindeer herders and conservation workers had finally been able to work so well together on a research project dealing with the controversial question of predators. He simply wanted to know if we felt the same about it.

Amul got the answer he was hoping for.

The magnificent white-tailed (sea) eagle can be recognized by its wedge-shaped tail, though it is only white in adults.

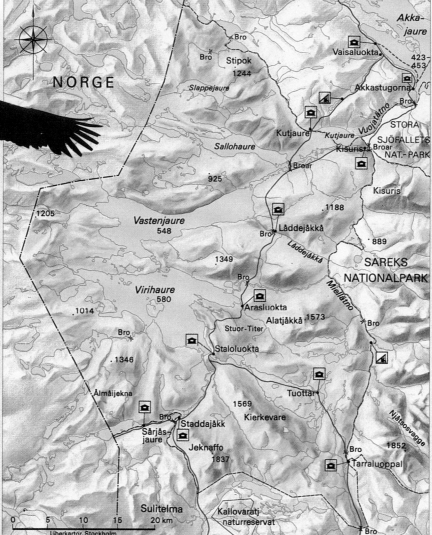

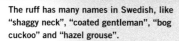

The ruff has many names in Swedish, like "shaggy neck", "coated gentleman", "bog cuckoo" and "hazel grouse".

Moor-king has "a pale and bloody mouth and bloodstained leaves", according to its discoverer, Olof Rudbeck the Younger.

Padjelanta, "The Higher Land", is a mountain world with an open, undulating feel to it. Globe-flower is a typical species of its herb-rich slopes.

Foundation	The park was established in 1962, to preserve a mountain landscape with numerous lakes and heaths. In 1967, Padjelanta was awarded the European Council's Diploma for Nature Conservation. Padjelanta is also included in the 940,000 hectares of the Laponian Area, which in 1996 was designated by UNESCO as a World Heritage Site.
Location	25 kilometres northwest of Kvikkjokk in the Municipality of Jokkmokk, Norrbotten County.
Area	The park's total area is 198,400 hectares (490,246 acres) of which 167,100 hectares are land and 31,300 hectares water surface. Of the land area, 1400 hectares consist of mountain birch forest, 1400 hectares glaciers, 1000 hectares marshland, 2000 hectares boulders and rock outcrops, and the remainder heaths and meadows.
Attractions	The open mountain landscape. The rich flora and bird life. The large lakes. The view from Jeknaffo.
Visiting Padjelanta	The park can be reached via the hiking trail, Padjelantaleden, from Kvikkjokk to the south or Ritsem in Stor Sjöfallet National Park to the north. From Ritsem there is boat transport across Lake Akkajaure to Änonjalme and Vaisaluokta. It takes at least a day to hike to the park boundary. Along the trail there are sleeping cabins at intervals of ten to twenty kilometres. There is a large research station at Staloluokta, which can be reached by plane from Ritsem or Vietas during the summer months.

The Sami chapel and belfry at Staloluokta.

Pieljekaise

Pieljekaise is a long ridge at the southern edge of Sweden's northern mountains. It lies like a lonely sentinel amidst a wide, birchclad transition zone that stretches between high mountains and a lower region of evergreen forest. The feature that gives the park its special character is the large expanse of unspoiled birch forest.

LANDSCAPE Mountain birch forest is a common, but nonetheless interesting, feature of many mountain landscapes. It benefits from the heavy snowfall that melts fairly late in the spring—a typical circumstance for Scandinavia, where the mountain weather is influenced by air from the Atlantic.

"The dark clouds gather, but beneath them Peljekaise lies magnificent and clear, looking out first on one and then on the other side of Laisvare and eventually turning so that one ear is hidden by the other."

KARL-ERIK FORSSLUND (1915)

The Saami name, Pieljekaise, means "ear mountain", because the twin peaks of the ridge resemble a human ear in profile. Although Pieljekaise is only 1100 metres above sea level, its barren summit rises very distinctly above the birch forest of the surrounding low terrain. The national park includes the southern section of the mountain ridge, plus an adjoining lowland of slightly rolling hills and numerous lakes to the south.

Only a small portion of the national park consists of bare mountains. The lower slopes and the entire lowland are covered by moraine soils which in many places form a landscape of low hills and ridges. The ridges can be up to one kilometre long and ten metres high. In the eastern section of the park, there are also some well-defined drumlins—long, graceful ridges of moraine that were formed around a core of rock under the last ice age glacier.

VEGETATION The greater part of Pieljekaise National Park is covered by birch forest, the unspoiled state of which had already attracted attention at the beginning of this century. The only areas of the park not covered by the forest are the open heaths on the upper slopes and peaks of the mountains.

Comparatively sparse stands of birch grow on mossy heaths with and an undergrowth of juniper, bilberry and crowberry. At many places on the lower mountain slopes there are also birch wood meadows with scatterings of aspen, bird cherry, grey alder and rowan trees. and an abundance of flowering plants. Near the large lake, Sädvajaure, there are some pines and spruces.

The distinguishing plant of the national park is the globe-flower. In the wooded meadows grow such tall plants as alpine sowthistle and melancholy thistle, angelica, northern wolfsbane, common valerian, wood stitchwort, wood cranesbill, meadowsweet and grass of Parnassus.

Opposite: Pieljekaise's fertile birch forests and many lakes, here Gaska-Bieljaure, make this a very inviting national park. Below: A pair of red-throated divers.

In a few places can also be found such hungry plants as purple saxifrage, yellow saxifrage, fragrant orchid and marsh arrow-grass.

Still visible at several places in the national park—Lake Aleb Tjallasjaure for example—are signs of the severe damage caused by infestations of the moth *Epirrita autumnata* during 1955-57. The moth larvae sometimes proliferate in such vast numbers that they can consume all the tree leaves over wide areas. The older wooded heaths suffer especially heavy damage, and the long-term effects— as evidenced by masses of dead trees—can dominate local landscapes for up to a hundred years afterward. The often younger trees of the wooded meadows are better able to recover by regenerating from their own roots.

ANIMAL LIFE   The area has a relatively diverse fauna, due to the varied and somewhat broken terrain, and to the mosaic of boulders, marshes, lakes and ponds. Common mammals of the park include the red fox, moose, stoat and hares. Present more sporadically are the pine marten, mink, bear, Arctic fox and wolverine. Typical smaller birds of the birch forest include the redpoll, brambling, willow warbler, ptarmigan and willow grouse. Larger species which nest along the lake shores are the common scoter, black-throated diver (Arctic loon) and goosander (common merganser).

THE HUMAN PRESENCE   Pieljekaise has long been an important reindeer-grazing area for the Semisjaur-Njarg Saami Village. There is a Saami dwelling-site at Lake Aleb Tjallasjaure. The most important Saami fishing grounds are in the three lakes along the park's southern boundary, Aleb Tjallasjaure, Vuoleb Tjallasjaure and Lutaure; they also fish the smaller lakes in the park's interior.

Above: **Garden angelica, with flies in attendance.**
Below: **The moose, or elk, lives throughout the Scandinavian mountain range, including Pieljekaise, which offers an abundant supply of forage.**

Northern wolfsbane was mentioned in 1673 in Johannes Schefferus's *Lapponia*: "There grows a grass there which the Lapps call 'Lapp boot grass', since its flowers are in appearance like the boots they wear."

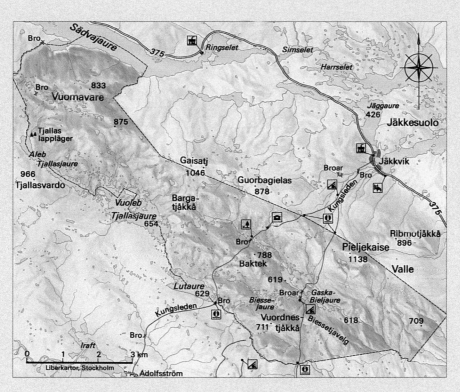

Globe-flower, or "doll of the valley", is a characteristic species of Pleljekaise.

Birch forest with a lush carpet of tall herbs.

Foundation A small section, 200 hectares, was established as a national park in 1909. In 1913 the park was expanded to its present dimensions. The purpose of the national park is to preserve an area of mountain birch forest in its natural state.

Location Six kilometres south of Jäkkvik, in the Municipality of Arjeplog, Norrbotten County.

Area The park's total area is 15,340 hectares (37,658 acres), of which 14,000 hectares are dry land and 1340 hectares water surface. The land area consists of 10,100 hectares birch forest, 700 hectares marshland and 3200 hectares bare mountains.

Attractions The mountain birch forest with its rich flora. The view from the peaks of Mt. Pieljekaise.

Visiting Pieljekaise The national park lies in a remote part of the mountains and receives few visitors, even though the national "Kungsleden" hiking trail passes through the area. The easiest approach to the park is via Kungsleden, along the six kilometres from Jäkkvikk to the north, or the nine kilometres from Adolfsström to the south. There is one sleeping shelter along Kungsleden.

A brooding dotterel, our most fearless and trusting mountain bird.

Sarek

The mountain landscape of Sarek National Park is the most dramatic in Sweden, and the least affected by human activity. There are jagged mountain peaks, immense glaciers, deep valleys and turbulent river rapids. Nowhere else in Europe is there such a vast expanse of monumental, uninterrupted wilderness.

LANDSCAPE Sarek lies in the northern section of the mountain range that stretches for 400 kilometres, all the way to Jämtland. The effects of ice ages on the mountain landscape are especially evident in Sarek. Glaciers have gouged deep U-shaped valleys from the massive bedrock, as well as the bowl-shaped cirques on the moun-

tain heights. The result is a series of steep cliffs and jagged crests which give the landscape a sharply defined profile.

This kind of mechanical erosion continues today, from the action of the one hundred or so glaciers in the area. Nevertheless, the national park includes the section of mountains in which erosion has had the least effect in levelling out the topography. The high central ridge of Sarek consists of hard rocks that have better resisted erosion than those of surrounding areas, both during and after the ice ages.

There are roughly 200 peaks within Sarek's boundaries, nearly all of them over 1800 metres above sea level. The park also includes six of Sweden's thirteen peaks with elevations in excess of 2000 metres.

The Rapaätno carries its load of glacial silt down the valley to Lake Laitaure. View to the east across the Rapadalen valley, from Kåtokvaratj.

The distances from the highest summits to the floors of adjacent valleys are extreme—up to 1300 metres in some cases. The park's most stately valley is Rapadalen, the central artery of Sarek. Its river, Rapaätno, drains some thirty glaciers and transports huge quantities of silt to Lake Laitaure at the valley entrance. This process has created the beautiful Rapa Delta, an expanding maze of channels and lagoons, marshes and solid ground. If the delta continues to expand at its present rate, the lake may be filled in a thousand years from now.

VEGETATION Boulders and bare mountains with sparse vegetation cover much of Sarek's surface. At the highest elevations grow lichens, mosses and dwarf willow, along with several species of grass and such flowering plants as glacier crowfoot. Further down, near the valleys, there is a ground cover of both grassy and bushy heaths, the

latter including juniper bushes, bilberry, dwarf birch and dwarf willow.

Spread out on the floors of the deepest valleys, particularly Rapadalen, are forests of mountain birch. At midsummer, the contrast between the windy, snow-flecked alpine heaths and the lush greenery of Rapadalen is striking. The valley's favourable local climate acts as a greenhouse, and its vegetation fairly bursts with life in the long summer daylight. In damp clearings amidst the birch forest, there are flowery meadows with such taller plants as globe-flower, northern wolfsbane, wood cranesbill and red campion.

ANIMAL LIFE Much of the park's animal life is concentrated in the valleys, which are crucial life-lines in the otherwise barren landscape. Rapadalen Valley is renowned for its exceptionally large moose, which wait until after the autumn hunting season is over

Above: View across Lake Laitaure towards Tjakkeli, at the mouth of the Rapaätno. Below: Subalpine birch forest in Rapadalen.

before moving out of the sheltering park. Sarek is thus home to the only moose herd in Sweden—and probably in Europe—which is essentially protected from hunting. Other large mammals of Sarek include the bear, wolverine, Arctic fox and lynx.

The birch forests and watercourses of the valleys are also the scene of the richest birdlife. Characteristic species include the willow warbler, brambling, bluethroat, yellow wagtail and pied flycatcher. The ponds and lagoons abound with such water birds as the teal, common scoter, wigeon and tufted duck. Common birds of the alpine heaths are the dotterel, golden plover, meadow pipit, Lapland bunting and ptarmigan. Also present are the long-tailed skua, golden eagle, rough-legged buzzard, merlin and gyrfalcon.

THE HUMAN PRESENCE There has probably never been a permanent human settlement in Sarek, but the area is used for summer grazing by the Saami villages of Sirka, Jåkkakaskas and Turopon. Sarek's rugged nature renders it less suitable for reindeer grazing than Padjelanta to the east. Research on glaciers and mountain formation processes has a long history in the park.

CLAES GRUNDSTEN

Sarek – a Swedish alpine world

"I wish," Dag Hammarskjöld once wrote, "that I could really describe how, during those days we wandered east down through Sarek, the light played on its stupendous instrument of rocky ridges and icy wastes, precipices and valleys."

After many treks in the mountains, he knew. Sarek can be a symphonic poem. A never-ending flood of light. But like Janus it has two faces. Just as you think you are really getting to know the peaks, they change shape. They slough their skin, with the help of the weather and the seasons. So you are never really done with Sarek.

One year brings me here during the different seasons. In January, my destination is Aktse, an old settlement site near the majestic entrance to the national park. I encounter a world that is deep-frozen. Midwinter is like an ice age, dark and with a cold that chills you to the marrow. But its meagre light is alluring. The mountainsides become kaleidoscopes as the sun plays hide-and-seek behind the summits. The few short hours of daylight ignite flares of red and yellow in the snow. At the same time, the temperature creeps steadily downwards. Visibility is good, and the weather cold, very cold. The landscape has a cruel beauty, and the silence gives me a philosophical peace.

"It takes time to develop an enduring love for a harsh, barren mountain landscape like Sarek."

Each day I survey the well-known trio of mountains that surrounds me, and their names have the rhythm of a children's rhyme as I repeat them: Skierfe – Nammatj – Tjakkeli. The place-names of Sarek should be savoured. They give the landscape an identity. Tell you that this is Sapmi, the old land of the Sami.

The mountains have jagged shapes, they seem to have been hewn out by the same architect. Tjakkeli and Nammatj resemble colossal building blocks, Skierfe the ridge of a roof. Ranged like the free-standing wings of a fairy-tale palace, they form the monumental gateway to Sarek. Below their precipices, perfectly framed, is the great Laitaure delta. Here the Rapadalen valley embarks on its meandering, deeply carved journey through the park. This is where Sarek begins.

In January, Sarek is a wilderness, in so far as anywhere still can be on this shrinking earth of ours. The fatefulness of the landscape permeates everything, giving me pleasure of the eccentric kind which only genuine hermits are capable of feeling. You become almost antisocial after a week here, and the sense of total isolation is reinforced every evening by the spectral curtains of the aurora.

Winter on the verge of spring is something altogether different, the vital coronation of the white half of the year. Now the time has come for a longer skiing tour through the central parts of the park. As I pass through the Kukkesvagge valley, my skis cross two fresh sets of bear tracks. I'm delighted that there are bears nearby. That's all I need to know. I could perhaps follow their trail, but I have other things to think about. Ascent.

My camp-site later that day looks across towards the famous peaks of Akka, and sundown is an exquisite performance on this alpine stage. The last rays of light make the crystal mountain glow with a subdued intensity that warms my soul. Akka is transformed into a dying camp-fire, and I watch the spectacle from outside my tent, reliving old memories.

There are no shortcuts to getting to know Sarek. If you want to befriend nature here, you have to lay up a store of experiences, year after year. It takes time to develop an enduring love

Above: **Glacier crowfoot grows at high altitudes in Sarek.**
Below: **The elk of Sarek have a reputation for coming in large sizes.**

A party of mountaineers ascending the ridge to the south peak of Sarektjåkkå gives some inkling of the monumental scale of the area. "Nowhere else in Sweden can you find yourself amid such wild topography as on Sarektjåkkå. Beyond the northern peak is a broad plateau, rising to new white-crested breakers in the distance," is how Claes Grundsten describes the scene.

for a harsh, barren mountain landscape like Sarek. The mountains can sometimes rebuff you. Often, they are swathed in fog, and floundering about up there in a fierce wind and under pressure, you may well wonder what it is that drives you on. Not even the people of the mountains themselves, the Sami, feel naturally drawn to the higher places.

Soaring mountains and menacing glaciers—it is this inhospitable but imposing scenery which, after all these years, I have

learnt to like the best in Sarek. A landscape with greater philosophical than biological interest.

The next day is radiant with energy. There isn't a cloud in the sky as I labour up the foothills of Sarektjåkkå. In the afternoon, I make the ascent of the mountain along its western ridge. It proves quite a demanding climb, over a carapace of rime, kneaded by the wind.

Nowhere else in Sweden can you find yourself amid such

wild topography as on Sarektjåkkå. On every side of the crest, there are breakneck drops of four to five hundred metres, and the storm-swept sea of mountain peaks seems to stretch away to infinity. To reach the northern summit of the massif, one of the corner towers of this fortress, you would have to balance on a narrow, elegant knife-edge, and the mere sight of it is enough to make anyone dizzy. Beyond the northern peak is a broad plateau, rising to new white-crested breakers in the distance.

It takes time to absorb the scene. And then you want time to talk to the gods, now that you are so near to heaven. I stay for a couple of hours, before returning to my tent at the foot of the western ridge.

In July, Rapadalen is once more my destination, and soon I can again see the solid backdrop of Skierfe, Nammatj and Tjakkeli, this time from the mountainside above the delta. Down below,

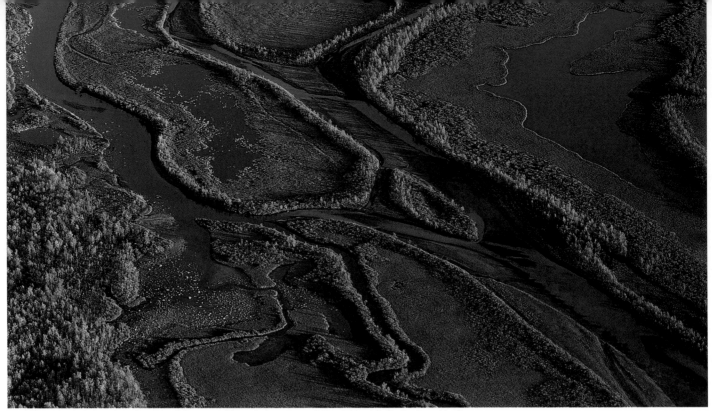

The twisting brushstrokes of the Rapaätno delta are reminiscent of a nature painting, laid out in the landscape to dry.

the terrain is impassable at this time of year, so I have to keep to the higher ground.

After a few days' toil, I reach Rapaselet, the heart of Sarek, where the Rapaätno divides into a tangle of braided channels. Here, nature has a pulse of its own. The river, huffing and puffing, carries its load of glacial silt and rock flour down the valley to deposit it on the delta, adding constantly to its fertile soil. Rapaselet, with its rich vegetation and deeply carved abyss, is a secluded paradise.

The valley landscape is like an old, furrowed face. Its secret lies in the contrast between the verdant profusion below and the black rocks above, and in the light, stage-managed by Piellorieppe to the south. On a clear day, this wild massif casts a spiky shadow on the valley below, before its outline is erased by the delicate summer-evening sun, which finds its way right down the valley and along the mountainsides.

Add to this the crisscrossing channels and lagoons on the flat valley floor, the colourful, bewildering delta with its purling river and its milk-white, sometimes turquoise-saturated water, its rich fauna of grazing, palmate-antlered elk, timid bears and restless wolverines – and you have a wilderness that lives in a timeless peace and of which you can never tire.

Rapadalen fires the imagination.

September has arrived. The best time for hiking in Sarek. The autumn colours are usually intense, mosquitoes are little more than a memory, the rivers and streams are at their lowest levels, and tourists are few and far between. I spend almost an entire day on top of Skierfe, in a crystal-clear air which is motionless, warm and cosseting. I wander back and forth along the abrupt edge of the precipice and gaze entranced at the delta below, where dazzling reflections dance on the serpentine twists and turns of the Rapaätno and whooper swans are gathering for their journey south.

The steep drop here is not for the faint-hearted. If you approach by the easy route, up the back of the mountain, you suddenly find yourself about to step out into empty space. Instinctively you retreat, before carefully approaching the edge again and finally, if you are not given to vertigo, abandoning yourself to the overwhelming view.

The birchwoods are a pale orange-yellow, still adorned with garlands of pea-green. But what if the autumn colours haven't quite got going yet, when it is one of those autumn days when the air is as clear as crystal and the smallest details of the landscape stand out razor-sharp? And when a golden eagle glides in over the mountain just twenty metres above my head, it is the culmination of an elusive feeling of confidence that leaves me first exalted, and then at peace.

To a Swede, the area which the eagle patrols is the very symbol of a national park. Vast, wild, rugged, and inaccessible. Harbouring a rich fauna and an astonishing mix of barren mountains and biologically productive valleys. An area such as this cannot be valued enough in our age of urbanization and environmental desecration. The sources of the doctrine which Sarek represents perhaps have to be sought far away in time and space.

In the nineteenth century, the American practical philosopher Henry David Thoreau expressed the sentiment: "In wildness is the preservation of the world". I dare say the golden eagle, if it could put its thoughts into words, would agree with that.

During the breeding season, the Arctic tern can be quite aggressive and repeatedly attack hikers and other intruders.

Of all the birds of prey, the gyrfalcon is best adapted to the harsh climate of the high mountains. It does not migrate in winter, being able to survive on a diet of ptarmigan. These two species are the only winter birds of the high mountain zone.

Like other mountain predators, the wolverine used to be hunted without quarter.

A group of walkers have set up camp overlooking Rapaselet in the heart of Sarek.

Foundation	The national park was established in 1909, in order to preserve an alpine landscape in its natural state. In 1967, Sarek was awarded the European Diploma for Nature Conservation. Sarek is also included in the 940,000 hectares of the Laponian Area, which in 1996 was designated by UNESCO as a World Heritage Site.
Location	Ten kilometres north of Kvikkjokk, in the Municipality of Jokkmokk, Norrbotten County.
Area	The national park covers 197,000 hectares (486,787 acres), of which 3900 hectares are water surface. The land area consists of 17,700 hectares mountain birch forest (which also includes small tracts of evergreen forest), 1700 hectares marshland, 14,800 hectares glaciers, and the remainder bare rocks and alpine heaths.
Attractions	The alpine landscape, with its jagged peaks, steep cliffs, glaciers and deep valleys. Rapadalen Valley, with its animal life and broad delta. The view over Rapadalen from Mount Skierfe.
Visiting Sarek	The national hiking trail, Kungsleden, runs through the southeastern tip of the park. Hikers may start out from Kvikkjokk and along Tarradalen Valley to the south, or from Saltoluokta to the north. Another approach is by boat from Ritsem, on the north shore of Lake Akkajaure, to the northern border of the park. Hiking in Sarek requires familiarity with alpine conditions, difficult terrain and rapidly changing weather. There are no sleeping facilities for tourists. There are only a few bridges, and crossing the many rivers may be difficult: Rain, or warm weather that accelerates glacial melting, may dramatically increase the flow of water. During winter, the risk of avalanches and severe snowstorms is great.

Skuleskogen

Skuleskogen National Park is a wild and majestic section of Ånger-manland's "High Coast", where the rolling hills of the Norrland forest meet the northern Baltic Sea. This roadless wilderness offers the visitor magnificent views over sea and forest, beautiful lakes, verdant spruce-clad valleys, and fascinating geological formations which, more clearly than anywhere else, demonstrate how much of modern Sweden has risen from the ancient sea.

LANDSCAPE The High Coast is part of the rolling hill landscape that dominates much of central Sweden. But it is only in Ångermanland that it reaches to the Baltic Sea, where it terminates in the only coastal cliffs in all of Sweden. Outside the western mountains, few other parts of the country display such an abrupt shift in elevation. The cliffs rise 300 metres from the shoreline and, just off shore, the water is very deep.

Since the retreat of the last ice age glacier, the land mass of the High Coast region has rebounded at a faster rate than anywhere else in Europe. Traces of the ice age waterline are now situated 286 metres above sea level, and wide rows of stone rubble formed by past wave action have been left on ledges that step down to the shoreline.

Remaining on some of the hilltops that rise above the highest former coastline are deposits of moraine that have escaped the waves of the ancient sea.

Skuleskogen National Park consists of numerous distinctive massifs and some deep, narrow valleys. The bedrock is of rapakivi, a reddish granite of which the largest deposits in Sweden are located at Skuleskogen. Rapakivi granite tends to erode into the kinds of regular patterns that are clearly visible in the park. The cliffs rise like giant stairways with nearly level steps.

Contributing to the dramatic character of Skuleskogen's terrain is a network of cracks and fissures in the bedrock. The most impressive of these is the gorge called Slåttdalsskrevan. It is 200 metres long and seven metres wide; with vertical walls nearly forty metres high. Another interesting phenomenon is the formation of grottoes from heaps of huge boulders.

There is more to Skuleskogen National Park than hills, forest and sea. Lying between the heights are some fifty lakes and ponds surrounded by spruce woods and marshland. The lakes are drained by several streams that ripple through the narrow valleys and down to the sea.

Opposite: The remarkable Slåttdalsskrevan fissure in Skuleskogen seems to have been created by a surgical incision straight down into the rock.
Below: The spruce forests in the valleys are strangely luxuriant in an otherwise rocky landscape.

Red rapakivi granite worn smooth by waves, sparse pine forest clinging to rocky ground, and an open, precipitous coastal landscape are characteristic features of Skuleskogen National Park.

VEGETATION At best, the hills washed nearly clean by the waves of the prehistoric sea can provide suitable conditions for meagre woods of pine. But growing in the valleys, where fine-grained soils have accumulated, are carpets of luxuriant spruce forest. The most remarkable woods in the park are those that grow thick as moss on the unwashed hilltops, providing the clearest evidence that the landscape was born from the sea.

The pines on rocky ground are small and twisted, but they can reach ages of up to 500 years. Due to excellent growing conditions in the fertile valleys, the park's spruces have now recovered from the heavy logging of the 19th century, and in many places have grown into stands of tall, broad-beamed trees.

The ranges of many plants usually associated with more southerly climes have their northern limit in Skuleskogen. They are relics from periods of warmer climate and include such tree species as hazel, lime and maple, as well as such plants as broad-leaved cinna and the relatively rare wood fescue. Oddly enough, some typically alpine species grow in isolated locations on the northern slopes of the highest hills; these include the hard fern, alpine sawwort, Scottish asphodel, and alpine catchfly.

Skuleskogen's most renowned species is the beardlichen *Usnea longissima,* which has become something of a symbol for all plants that have suffered the effects of modern logging. This lichen has disappeared from large parts of Sweden's forests, but still grows abundantly in the damp spruce woods of Skuleskogen.

ANIMAL LIFE Skuleskogen's animal life is dominated by species usually found in evergreen forests, especially those which benefit from the presence of older, undisturbed trees. They include the grey-headed, black, lesser spotted, great spotted and three-toed wood-peckers. Other common species are the game birds, capercaillie, black grouse, hazelhen and willow grouse, as well as such perching birds as the wren, wood warbler, blackcap and several varieties of tit. Characteristic mammals include the moose, roe deer, lynx, badger, stoat, pine marten, mink, mountain hare, red squirrel and assorted small rodents.

THE HUMAN PRESENCE Skuleskogen's rugged and wild terrain has discouraged permanent settlement, but there are many traces of past human activity. The oldest historical remains are graves from the Bronze Age (1500-500 B.C.) The graves are in the form of stone cairns that were erected along the coastline of that time, but which are now 40–50 metres above sea level due to the continuing land elevation.

For many centuries, the forest has been used for grazing and the marsh meadows for hay-making. Summer grazing came to an end at the beginning of the 1900s. There was intensive logging during the 19th century, but all traces of that period are gradually disappearing.

"...if we were for no other purpose to pay heed to the things that are created, then we should in truth do so to honour and glorify the Creator; since in every plant, and every animal and stone, we can see an extraordinary masterpiece, which we find in no other body."

LINNAEUS

Kerstin Ekman

KERSTIN EKMAN

Skuleskogen – the wildest of forests

No woodland is as wild as the Forest of Skule. It lies between the high hills and the coast, below the arid, alien landscape north of the forest country. Nowhere else is the Bothnian Sea so deep, nor do the islands have such precipitous peaks. The sea is a cold autumnal blue and the red granite glows unquenchably beneath the attacks of the waves against the rocky precipices. The forest grows on hillsides and on the steep sides of the dark river ravines. The slopes are covered with moorland and the streams leap along from waterfall to waterfall. Everywhere are fields of scree and stones, deep clefts and heavy sharp-edged rocks. Only the still clearwater lochans are smooth-surfaced, but their depth chills the eye.

Strands of time run through the forest. The high fields of scree are solidified waves of stone, long swells of unmoving time. Tall trees, once whispering in the wind, have sunk into the peatbogs, where the marshy pools are fermenting a brew of time. Here and there, flowering woodland penetrates the darkness of the spruces and the sea of stones, forming wedges of broad-leaved trees, fragrant night-flowering plants and humming frail-winged insects. There, the noble trees are singing. The leaves of linden and hazel are dancing in a gentler wind and their roots send fibrils into a richer soil than the meagre ground under the spruces. It is forgotten woodland, flowering in borrowed time.

A large crack has opened up in one of the rockfaces. The stone has fallen down or eroded away, leaving behind a cleft with perpendicular edges. It is no wider than the gap between two people talking. Deep inside it the dark is lifeless; there are only stones and shadows.

A mountain-side with such a deep crack, visible from far away and unchanging within human memory, must be a mark or a sign. And if it is not a sign, if it means nothing, is that not even more thought-provoking? In any case, it is a fact that the cleft in the mountain, so straight and bottomlessly deep, existed long before any brain which could formulate thoughts and use images for its own purposes. Nobody knows if the immense crack found a purpose for the thoughts, as they began to swarm around the mountain. Nobody knows. The thoughts flutter like feathered moths inside people's heads, but the crack stays where she is, cutting a gash through time.

Scattered tussocks of grass brighten up the meagre, rocky terrain.
Top: Alpine catchfly still survives in Skuleskogen, along with several other typical mountain plants.

People have always tried to slash and burn their way into the forest. And when it proved resilient, when even the goats failed to tear the bark off the trees, they tried to control it by naming. They found everything malevolent in the forest: stinkweed and snakeberry, troll's grapes, corpse fungus and dwarf bladder.* The plants which neither stank nor stung nor killed they named according to who fed on them: hare's sorrel, eagle fern, henberry, goat's lily and bee flower, elkwort and bear's kale. For some, playfulness and for others, plain practicality.

The rest became known as grass to most people, but there were those who named also the useless and the lovely ones: star sedge and goldenrod, king's sceptre, lesser rosemary, woodstar and gnome's rose, such were their names.

But the forest just grew and flowered. It flowered with senseless frenzy, remote from their names, and some wanderers came all the way, down into the deepest hollows under the stones and the darkness of marshland pools, and on to the steep silent braes of the lochs and they named the strange growths in these places and called them comb fern and mountain sloucher, grove grass and rough horsetail. But it was not enough. The forest flowered on heedlessly, long after they had been silenced, roots twisting through their gaping mouths, it flowered known and named only by those who hummed and clicked and twittered, by the rustle of wings and rattle of claws and thud of antlers against treetrunks.

> *"The forest flowered on … known and named only by those who hummed and clicked and twittered, by the rustle of wings and rattle of claws and thud of antlers against treetrunks."*

* Footnote, see page 151

Left: A sunbeam falls through the forest canopy like a spotlight onto that little songstress, the wren.
Below: Large raised beaches of cobbles recall where the waves of the sea broke after the ice age.

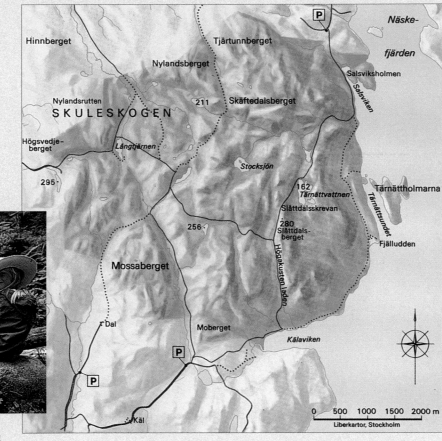

Visitors to Skuleskogen can enjoy a very varied walk through spruce forests, along streams and across granite plateaux and raised cobble beaches.

Hard fern prefers to grow in gloomy, damp forest terrain.

The threatened beard lichen *Usnea longissima* cannot cope with modern forestry. In Skuleskogen, however, the species has survived.

Early in the spring, the bubbling of blackcocks rises from the mires of the "High Coast".

Foundation	The national park was established in 1984, in order to preserve a coastal forest landscape with steep hills, rocky outcrops and fissure valleys. The area is to remain undisturbed, so that plant and animal life may develop naturally.
Location	Approximately forty kilometres south of Örnsköldsvik, in the municipalities of Örnsköldsvik and Kramfors, Västernorrland County.
Area	The total area is 2950 hectares (7290 acres), of which 2680 hectares are dry land. The land area consists of 1514 hectares evergreen forest, 42 hectares broad-leaved forest, nine hectares wooded marshes, 116 hectares open marshes, one hectare meadowland, and 998 hectares rocky outcrops, boulders and stone rubble.
Attractions	The till-capped hills. Large areas of rocky outcrops and stone rubble. The gorge of Slåttsdalsskrevan. Broad views over sea and forest. Verdant valleys of spruce forest with interesting flora.
Visiting Skuleskogen	Signs on European Highway E4 show the way to the national park. There is an access road from the south via Käl, and from the north via Näske. The Skule Nature Centre off Highway E4 provides an introduction to the park's human and natural history. There are 30 kilometres of hiking trails, as well as three sleeping cabins and two shelters that are open year round.

Stenshuvud

Stenshuvud National Park is located on the southeast coast of Sweden, in the part of Skåne known as Österlen. It is a place where coastal hills, shady broad-leaved woods, pastoral heaths and inviting beaches unite to form an exquisite landscape. The national park possesses great biological diversity and the exotic character of more southerly climes.

LANDSCAPE The rolling landscape of northern and eastern Skåne differs markedly from the broad flatlands in its southern and south-eastern tracts. The hills are landforms called horsts, which were created by movements in the earth's crust 600 million years ago, when fractures in the bedrock resulted in the formation of ridges such as Söderås and Linderödsås.

Stenshuvud ("Stone Head") is located on the shore of Hanö Bay, southeast of Linderödsås. It has a steeper profile than the other heights of Skåne, and is felt to be the hard core of a once larger formation of which the greater portion has weathered away. Its steep slopes and its abrupt meeting with the Baltic Sea give Stenshuvud a more dramatic character than the other, more gently-shaped ridges of the region.

The crown of Stenshuvud is 97 metres above sea level, and is the park's dominant landmark. Its northwest flank is very steep, with bare cliffs that plunge straight down into the forest below. In other directions, the ridge slopes more gently—except to the east, where the cliffs rise steeply from the sea.

The park consists primarily of shady woods, open heaths and meadows on level or gently sloping terrain. The heaths and mead-

Right: The sandy beach comes to a halt where Stenshuvud Hill meets the sea.
Below: The goldfinch is lively and melodious. In the south of Europe it has long been hunted and kept as a cage-bird.

"Heather is one of the most companionable of plants and yet also one of the most intrusive. In many places it is this plant which essentially determines the appearance of the entire landscape," the botanist C. F. Nyman wrote some 130 years ago.

ows contrast sharply with the soft contours of the adjoining sandy beaches. Through sandy areas of the park's interior wind two rivers; the larger of the two, the north branch of the Rorum River, has carved out a ravine nearly ten metres deep.

North of Stenshuvud ridge are deposits of stone rubble which mark the location of the shoreline during various geological periods. The oldest of these ancient shorelines lies 32 metres above the current sea level.

VEGETATION The area's long history of human activity has left its mark on Stenshuvud, and the national park is rich in biological diversity. The traditional nature of the heaths and meadows is being maintained by active measures, but the woods are being left to develop naturally.

The woods have something of a southern character due largely to the presence of hornbeam, a tree species which in Sweden forms significant stands only in Skåne, Blekinge and Öland. The stand at Stenshuvud is one of the largest in the country; the ridge slopes and the northern section of the park are nearly covered in hornbeam. The next most common species is beech. Other tree species typical of the area are lime (linden), oak, elm and ash.

Every spring, the broad-leaved woods put on a magnificent display of flowers, including wood anemone, hepatica, yellow anemone, yellow star of Bethlehem and several varieties of corydalis. A bit later blossom yellow archangel, woodruff, ramsons, coralroot

bittercress and many other shade-tolerant plants. The spring floral display is intense but short-lived. When the dense foliage of the tree canopy spreads its cloak of summer shadow, the ground cover becomes a carpet of uniformly green leaves. Then, such hungry shade-tolerant plants as wood barley, giant fescue and wood millet are among the most noteworthy species of the broad-leaved forest floor.

The southern character of Stenshuvud's woodland is accentuated by the ivy that winds along the ground and high up in the trees. Another climbing plant, honeysuckle, is common in the dense woods of the rocky slopes facing the sea. The characteristic trees of this drier habitat are gnarled oaks. A bit inland from the heights, a damp valley offers a different sort of forest habitat, including some enchanted fens where ferns grow thick around the knotty bases of alder trees.

Like the broad-leaved woods, the heaths change character with the seasons. In early spring, great quantities of pasque-flower grow on the grassy heaths. But these areas, with their dry soils and tall junipers, bloom most intensely during mid-summer with such yellow flowers as helichrysum, lady's bedstraw, biting stonecrop and various hawkweeds and hawksbeards. The heather-dominated heaths begin to display their full colour toward the end of summer.

The vegetation of the heaths and meadows has adapted to centuries of grazing. The same is true of Stenshuvud's meadows, both dry and damp, which have a much richer flora of orchids and other

Above: Stenshuvud's alder carr is a distinctive habitat of an almost tropical character.
Below: The green tree frog is the only Swedish frog which has sticky pads on its toes to enable it to climb from leaf to leaf.

flowers than the heaths. Although the meadows comprise only a small part of the park's total area, they include the sites for most of its ca. 600 vascular plants.

ANIMAL LIFE The varied habitats of Stenshuvud provide the conditions for a diverse and prolific animal life. The roe deer, red fox, wild rabbit, red squirrel and badger are among the mammals that can be seen, in addition to the park's symbol, the dormouse. Also present are the agile and common tree frogs, and all seven of Sweden's reptile species. Large butterflies comprise one of the best-represented animal groups in the Stenshuvud area. Of Sweden's roughly 1000 species, 445 have been sighted in the park.

Included in the rich birdlife of the broad-leaved woods are many melodious songbirds such as the thrush nightingale, icterine warbler, scarlet rosefinch (grosbeak), blackcap and garden warbler, and even such rarities as the marsh warbler and golden oriole. The linnet, goldfinch, red-backed shrike, tawny pipit and partridge are among the species that can be seen in the open areas.

THE HUMAN PRESENCE Stenshuvud has been used by humans ever since the region was inhabited following the last ice age. The remains of a fortress from the Late Iron Age can be seen on the highest ridge. The area was used for grazing for centuries. The woods of today have reclaimed the once-open land during the past hundred years. Krivareboden is a fishing hut from the 18th century, still in use.

JAN DANIELSON

Stenshuvud – blue hill and green

For centuries, Stenshuvud was known as the Blue Hill. Seafarers from the north and from the south saw it as a landmark, a stooping dragon keeping guard over its secrets. In ports around the Baltic, the story went that it was the home of a giant and his wife. At one spot, there were two pillars of rock, fashioned by nature. They were known as the Giant's Gate, and were said to mark the entrance to his garden. If you happened to point your telescope between them, your ship was doomed. It was best to keep far enough away to make sure the Blue Hill remained blue.

Many people saw the hill, but few had set foot on it.

Now all that has changed. Ships navigate by signals from satellites which spin in rapid orbit around the earth. Skippers know their exact position at any time. The Blue Hill is no longer needed as a landmark. Today's helmsmen may perhaps cast an indifferent glance in its direction from time to time, but on the whole they keep their eyes firmly fixed on their instrument panels.

Few people see the hill from out at sea, but many approach it from the landward side. Stenshuvud has become the Green Hill. A place for a close encounter with nature, beautiful and mystical. We don't want to know our exact position at any time; we're searching for secrets.

The path into the national park from Hällevik to the north of the hill is a narrow tunnel through an impenetrable cypress forest. A brown tangle of twigs, a heavy, dull green. In the middle of the tunnel, a sweet chestnut has pierced a hole in the darkness and spreads its crown like a green funnel. Lanky specimens of touch-me-not balsam gratefully soak up the little light that trickles down to the ground.

All the trees here, though, are exotic guests from remote corners of the earth. They seem to be somewhere else, although they are very much here, their roots firmly anchored in the soil, and branches dreaming of the forests where they really belong.

The path winds its way through cobble-stone terrain, closer and closer to the hill. The forest has an exotic compactness, it is a world of green. The green of the moss-covered rocks, the green of the crooked hornbeam trunks, decorated like maypoles with small, leafy shoots, the green of the honeysuckle that entwines itself around the young trees in the glades, the green of light carefully filtered through thin layers of chlorophyll. Even the birdsong seems green: the accelerando of the wood warbler, the rippling of the blackcap.

Above: **Beyond the low-growing forest and the juniper heath looms Stenshuvud Hill. Far left: From the deciduous woods behind Stenshuvud comes the fragrance of honeysuckle.**

Along the path, on a summer night, you might find one of Sweden's rarest beetles, which Linnaeus honoured with the name *Carabus intricatus*, "the most beautiful of all". Gleaming blue, purple—and green. Not many people have seen it.

Suddenly, you are in a wood unlike anything you have ever seen. Thick, hairy muscles squeeze the stems of the trees in their iron grasp, so tight that they seem to fuse with the bark. Hirsute snakes which, under cover of darkness, have wound their way up into the trees and, surprised by daylight, have frozen to avoid discovery.

This is ivy, seeking support and help in life. As it journeys upwards towards the light, its glossy foliage swells, following the branches out to the finest twigs at their tips. The trees are green, not only with their own leaves, but in part with borrowed plumes, a kind of earnestly shiny, dark green vestment which, especially in winter when the trees' own leaves have long since been shed, has a strange eeriness.

The path continues down in the valley, which is different yet again. Here the eye is tricked by an illusory world, upside down, nervously inconstant and shimmering. An alder carr perched in inky black water, each tree reigning over its own miniature island, surrounded by its fern and horsetail subjects; its reflections are razor-sharp, with intersecting diagonals and a tangle of branches disappearing dizzily beyond the toecaps of its boots. Then suddenly a flake of bark drops onto the water, a

The meadow to the south of Stenshuvud Hill. In spring and early summer it puts on a fine display of flowers.

mosquito emerges from the depths, and this make-believe world is shaken to its foundations.

The three summits of the hill resemble low reefs of grey rock a few tens of metres apart, in a sea of green whose breakers splash up among their crevices as grass and moss. Ninety-seven metres below is the other sea, the blue sea, marked off from the green by a golden strip of sand.

But what are those creatures scattered over the heath to the south? Dark figures, some tall and slender like medieval knights in broad capes, others big and shaggy like prehistoric cattle. Knights and cattle alike are junipers, old, dry, stubborn and surly. They have to be, to survive on a heath that offers no shelter from the burning sun or the icy winds.

"...a sea of green whose breakers splash up among the crevices of the reefs as grass and moss."

The junipers are not the only inhabitants of the heath. They share it with thyme and pinks, whose overpowering fragrance can spread right across the hill if the season and the wind are right.

A view reveals no secrets. But the secrets are there. Paths of a different kind to those trodden by man run through the vegetation of this green eminence. The thickets of bramble, blackthorn and glaucous dog rose, gorse, guelder rose and juniper are the home of the bright-eyed dormouse. Averse to ground travel, he prefers to make his way through their maze of branches, thorns and leaves.

Other pathways are to be found high in the spreading crowns of the trees, where small green tree frogs journey in the late summer. With the sticky disks on their feet, they are uniquely equipped to get around and colonize new patches of water along their windswept migration routes.

Exotic butterflies and moths sometimes cross the sea to Stenshuvud. Painted lady, red admiral and death's head hawk-moth visit from southern Europe almost every year. Occasionally, a purple emperor has been seen sailing over the treetops. No one knows what draws them here. Perhaps, to them, Stenshuvud is still the Blue Hill?

One perfectly still, sun-steeped summer dawn, as I approached the hill with Thomas Hansson, the park warden, during a live broadcast of a radio nature programme, I suddenly heard the desperate cry of the technician through my headphones: "You're fading, I can't hear a thing!" As we got closer still, everything went dead. Perspiration trickled from our brows.

We hadn't reckoned with Giant Sten. The hill, combined with the strong solar radiation, had upset all our calculations. So we had to change our plans and take the path over the heath, among the junipers and wild roses, the hawthorn and blackthorn.

On a normal summer's day, the dawn chorus can be deafening here. The cascading scales of the thrush nightingale can seem almost painfully loud, drowning out the whitethroat's chatter, the rattling of the lesser whitethroat and the courteous "Pleased to see you, pleased to see you..." of the scarlet grosbeak. Up in the massive oaks we should also have heard the soft fluting of the golden oriole and the insistent cooing of the stock dove.

But this morning we could hear none of this. Not so much as a leaf moved in the still air. It was as if Stenshuvud, in all its fair beauty, had been encased in glass. I felt my mouth filling with desert sand, my tongue swelling up, my voice becoming hoarse and strained. The warden, normally not at a loss for words, fell more silent than he had ever been under the curse that was upon us.

This morning was too beautiful, too hot. All the creatures of the hill were silenced and paralysed. There were no butterflies fluttering across the meadow. No adders basking on the rocks. No lizards seeking out the warmth around the juniper roots. Nature was inaccessible. We were in paradise, but unable to convey all its glory.

The early birds who tuned in to the programme that Saturday morning never really did find out what a rich and interesting place Stenshuvud is. But they did perhaps get some inkling of the power he still holds—Giant Sten. The Blue Hill. The Green Hill.

Ramsons flowers profusely in June in the national park's deciduous woods.

Ivy completely engulfs some trees, in this case a beech.

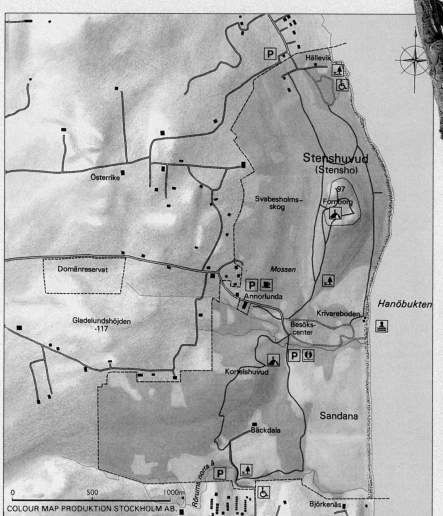
COLOUR MAP PRODUKTION STOCKHOLM AB.

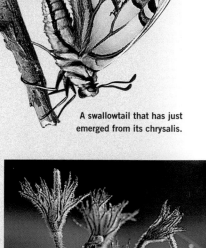
A swallowtail that has just emerged from its chrysalis.

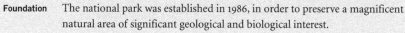
Pasque-flower retains the evening light in its hairy fruits.

The sand lizard is one of Stenshuvud's many reptiles.

Foundation	The national park was established in 1986, in order to preserve a magnificent natural area of significant geological and biological interest.
Location	About 2.5 kilometres southwest of Kivik in the Municipality of Simrishamn, Skåne County.
Area	The national park includes 380 hectares (939 acres), of which 327 hectares are land. 214 hectares of the land area consist of broad-leaved woods, 23 hectares of cropland and orchards, four hectares of beaches, and 86 hectares of meadows, heaths and open fens.
Attractions	The view from the crest of Stenshuvud ridge. The broad-leaved woods, heaths, meadows, and the inviting beaches. The rich plant and animal life. The nature centre with its displays.
Visiting Stenshuvud	Stenshuvud is near Kivik in south-east Skåne. The main entrance can be reached by car from S. Mellby. The northern entrance is at Hällevik. A visitor centre at the main entrance informs about the area's human and natural history. Trails lead through the park and to the summit of Stenshuvud.

Stora Sjöfallet

Stora Sjöfallet National Park preserves a section of northern Scandinavia's alpine landscape, with imposing mountain ridges, deep valleys, boulder-strewn high plains, ancient pine forest, and the magnificent Akka Massif, known as "The Queen of Lapland".

LANDSCAPE When visiting the park, it is worth recalling botanist Sten Selander's expressive description of the falls, where "chaos reigned in all its primeval frenzy". Even if the central section of the area and its famous waterfall have been exploited and are no longer included in the national park, the wide-ranging mountains still retain valuable natural features.

The park is the country's third largest, and lies at the centre of Sweden's largest protected area—the 9000 square kilometres which also include Sarek, Muddus and Sjaunja national parks. Stora Sjöfallet forms the core of the area, and particularly its southern section has great similarities to the wild mountains of neighbouring Sarek.

Stora Sjöfallet National Park consists of two roughly equal parts lying north and south of the Akkajaure Reservoir. The northern part consists of a long mountain ridge with several peaks that runs between the reservoir and the Teusa Valley. The highest peaks of the Kallaktjåkkå Massif are over 1800 metres above sea level; its heights have been gouged

> *"When we suddenly caught sight of the falls, close upon us, we felt an urge to crouch down as if seeking cover. Chaos reigned in all its primal frenzy – yet at the same time it was law-bound and majestically beautiful. When we finally departed, dazed and deafened by the thundering water, and continued up the mountainside, the whole of the alpine landscape suddenly seemed strangely tame."*
> STEN SELANDER

and sharpened by geological forces that have left a series of glacial cirques. The deep and narrow Teusa Valley, which forms the park's northern boundary, is one of the most stunningly beautiful valleys in the Swedish mountains.

South of the Akkajaure Reservoir, the mountain terrain is more varied. The glaciers and sheer peaks of Mount Akka reach elevations above 2000 metres. The Akka Massif has the steepest vertical rise in the country—1500 metres from crest to base—and its solitary seclusion from other mountains accentuates its majestic profile.

East of Mount Akka at an elevation of 900 metres is the broad, high plain of Kassalako, with its many lakes. The plain is barren as an

Akka is described in Selma Lagerlöf's _The Wonderful Adventures of Nils Holgersson_. To see the mountain in the red glow of an autumn sunset is a powerful experience.

Arctic waste and very difficult to traverse, due to the massive boulder accumulations. Southeast of Kassalako, the land slopes down to the Kukkesvagge Valley, which runs for over ten kilometres and forms an almost perfectly straight boundary between Stora Sjöfallet and Sarek national parks.

One of the Swedish mountains' most beautiful and scientifically interesting ice-age deltas lies west of the Akka Massif. The delta is built up of huge deposits of sand and gravel, which form a series of terraces at several levels and terminate in a fifty-metre-high sand bluff. The higher terraces are dotted by a number of basins which were formed when ice blocks embedded in the gravel melted away.

VEGETATION The vegetation of Stora Sjöfallet is quite sparse, due to a shortage of calcium in the bedrock. The most interesting feature is the beautiful ancient pine forest along the road to Sjöfallet and in the valley north of the former falls. This is the western limit of Sweden's evergreen forest, its silvery dead trees and broad-beamed ancient survivors forming a striking visual border along the base of the mountain landscape. The forest covers 2500 hectares, and the most venerable pines are over 500 years old.

At the park's lower elevations, there are large areas of mountain birch. Most of the birches are located on mossy heaths; but on the more fertile soils of the Teusa Valley and the southern slopes facing the Akkajaure Reservoir, there are birch woods with luxuriant undergrowth. In the park's easternmost section, near the Kierkau Massif, there are lush growths of mountain avens and Arctic rhododendron, or Lapland rosebay.

ANIMAL LIFE The animal life of the park has been adversely affected by the construction of hydroelectric facilities, road-building, etc.

Yellow saxifrage grows in the inhospitable Arctic environment of the park.

But such larger mammals as the moose, wolverine, bear and lynx are present in the park. There are relatively few water birds; but there is a normal assortment of smaller alpine species, including the snow bunting, Lapland bunting, wheatear, golden plover and ptarmigan.

THE HUMAN PRESENCE Stora Sjöfallet National Park was established in 1909, in order to preserve the famous waterfall and the lakes that feed the Stora Lule River. But the park's name is now misleading: In 1919, the Swedish Parliament decided to remove the entire lake system above the falls from the park, in order to permit the construction of an extensive hydroelectric complex. Akkajaure is now an artificial lake.

As elsewhere in the mountains, the Stora Sjöfallet area has long been used by the Saami for reindeer herding. It is part of the Sirka and Sörkaitum Saami villages' summer grazing land.

Stora Sjöfallet National Park has everything from sharp peaks rising from high mountain heaths to the twisted sculptures of dead trees in its virgin pine forests.

Ptarmigans at rest.

A cold spring rises from the bedrock in Stora Sjöfallet National Park, watched over by the conical peak of Slugga outside the park boundary.

The Arctic fox has declined throughout Sweden. Forty years ago it could be found even in the south of the country.

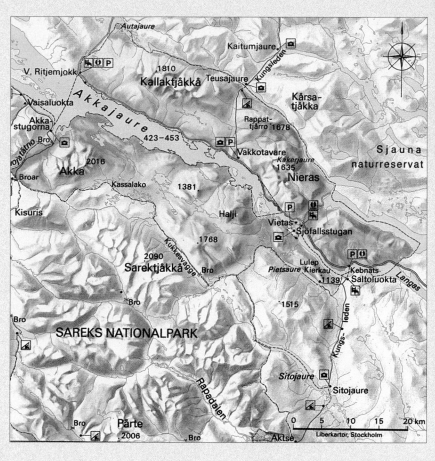

One of the twin falls in the Luomijåkka Stream.

Foundation	The national park was established in 1909, originally for the purpose of preserving the waterfall and the lake sources of the Stora Lule River. The present function of the park is to preserve a northern Scandinavian alpine landscape in its natural state. Stora Sjöfallet is also included in the 940,000 hectares of the Laponian Area, which in 1996 was designated by UNESCO as a World Heritage Site.
Location	Ninety kilometres west of Porjus, in the municipalities of Gällivare and Jokkmokk, Norrbotten County.
Area	The national park includes 127,800 hectares (313,323 acres), of which 118,700 hectares are land and 9100 hectares are water surface. Of the land area, 28,100 hectares are mountain birch forest, 2600 hectares pine forest, 700 hectares marshland, 200 hectares connected with buildings and hydroelectric facilities, and the remainder heaths and bare mountains.
Attractions	The majestic Akka Massif. The primeval pine forest at Vietas. The magnificent Teusa Valley. The Akka Terraces.
Visiting Stora Sjöfallet	The national park can be reached by a road from Porjus, which passes Vietas and continues west along the north shore of the reservoir to the park's western boundary. Accommodation is available at the Vietas tourist facility, and at cabins along the service road. The Kungsleden hiking trail passes through the park's northern section. There are no hiking trails or sleeping accommodations in the southern section of the park.

Store Mosse

Store Mosse in the highlands of Småland is the largest Swedish
marsh complex south of Lapland. It extends over an area of nearly
10,000 hectares, and forms a landscape that has retained its
pristine character. It is also the site of Lake Kävsjön, one of the
best-known bird habitats in Sweden.

LANDSCAPE Outside the mountains, there are only a few places in
Sweden which have been preserved in their natural state. In southern
Sweden, it is primarily the marshlands that have survived intact, as
they have been less interesting for human exploitation. Sweden's
undisturbed marshes represent a natural asset which, up till now, has
not been fully appreciated. The situation is even worse in other
European countries, where marshland has been subjected to much
greater human impact—or completely destroyed.

Store Mosse rests on an unusually level plateau of gneiss bedrock.
The highest and lowest elevations within the park vary by no more
than ten metres.

The history of Store Mosse begins with Fornbolmen, a glacial lake
which once covered the entire area.

> *"The Creator sought not only
> utility, but beauty too, for he was
> also an artist."*
>
> AUGUST STRINDBERG (1907)

After the heavy glacier of the last ice
age retreated to the north about
8000 years ago, the landmass began
to rise again, displacing much of
the water in Fornbolmen. The ex-
posed seafloor was covered with sand, which the winds formed into
dunes during a period of dry climate. This is believed to be the
explanation for Store Mosse's extensive and somewhat unusual
conglomeration of sand hills and low, winding ridges.

The formation of the marshes began during a period of wet
climate some 6000 years ago. The sandy ground became waterlogged and depleted of oxygen. As a result, partially-decomposed
plant matter accumulated in ever-increasing layers of peat, which
now have a combined thickness of between three and seven metres.

VEGETATION There are two main types of marsh in Store Mosse,
which can be roughly described as elevated bogs and low-lying fens.
The bogs grow above the surrounding terrain through the accumulation of plant matter, and have a slightly domed appearance. The
only water they receive is precipitation, as a result of which the
vegetation is sparse. In addition to several varieties of *Sphagnum*
moss, typical plants of the bogs are heather, cross-leaved heath, bog
rosemary, cranberry, hare's-tail, cotton-grass and dwarf birch.

Southern Sweden's biggest mire complex stretches
into the distance like an interminable sea of peat.

"And when the cranberries are ripe, they are pulled down onto the moss by their weight, and look almost as if they belong to it entirely" (C. F. Nyman, 1867).

The low-lying fens receive nutrient-rich water from surrounding areas, and have therefore a more luxuriant vegetation. Growing in abundance on Björnekullakärret, the botanically-interesting fen in the park's southern section, are such orchids as the marsh helleborine, fragrant orchid and narrow-leaved (Pugsley's) marsh orchid.

Although the park's solitary stunted pines are no taller than a man's height, they can be up to several hundred years old. But most of the marshland is treeless, and so broad that it is sometimes difficult to make out the edge of the forest on the opposite side.

A surprisingly dry and pleasant opportunity for a stroll is offered by the pine-clad sandbanks that wind far out on the marshes in the southern section of the park. In former times, farming was conducted on the solid moraine of the "marsh islets", Lövö and Svanö. The cheerful pastoral landscape, with its meadows and its leafy groves, is now being looked after, and provides a luxuriant contrast to the bleakness of the surrounding marshland.

ANIMAL LIFE Lake Kävsjön has long been renowned for its exceptional birdlife. It is an important nesting site for ducks and wading birds, and for the black-headed gull, of which there is a large colony. Among nesting ducks are the mallard, teal, wigeon, pochard and shoveler. The most common wading birds are the lapwing, curlew, snipe, redshank and wood sandpiper. There are also some species that are usually associated with more northerly latitudes, including the greenshank, broad-billed sandpiper and jacksnipe.

The characteristic birds of the marshes are the golden plover, meadow pipit and the crane; the last-named visits the park in large numbers during migration. Other birds which nest on the marshes are the Slavonian grebe, whooper swan, Arctic loon (black-throated diver), raven and short-eared owl. Altogether, some 100 bird species nest in the park.

THE HUMAN PRESENCE Farmers have worked and lived on the two "marsh islets" of Lövö and Svanö from the 1600s to the beginning of this century. Other areas have been affected by drainage ditches, the lowering of lakes, and peat-cutting. A road and a railway cross the park at its narrowest point. But most of the area lacks all trace of human influence, thus forming a wilderness that is quite remarkable for southern Sweden.

STEFAN EDMAN

Store Mosse – southern Sweden's greatest wilderness

wilight. A raw chill. Icy puddles on the winding gravel road. I turn off the engine. The silence bounces towards me, and with it the sour odours from the black "moat" fringing the bog. Not a sign of life. But I know there is life here, hidden away in the yellowed grass: thousands of insects over-wintering, the mosquito swarms of next summer. Flies. Butter-flies and moths.

This is Store Mosse, on a November day in 1995. A fantastic fossil landscape wedged between the asphalt highways and ur-ban clamour of the modern age. One of southern Sweden's few wildernesses, as good as untouched by human hands.

A hooded crow rasps from a stunted pine beneath an over-cast sky. Warily, I step out onto the hummocks of the bog, and take a flying leap over the wateriest hollow. Black grouse drop-pings, and a few feathers, are scattered over the moss.

The cranberry is very much in evidence here, that now al-most forgotten cousin of the bilberry and cowberry. I follow its stems, with their small, leathery leaves, as they twist into the

distance, and my gaze alights on a clump of ripe berries, pink droplets brightening up the greyness of the day. This is the time to pick them, in the late autumn, and preferably after a frosty night has made them less sour to the palate. They make a cordial which the Smålanders of old recommended as a cure for fevers and colds. Our Bronze Age ancestors are said to have brewed their drinks from cranberries and bog myrtle. I savour the refreshing taste of the berries, and travel back three thou-sand years in time. Isn't that a bronze lur sounding in the dusk over there, towards Svartegöl?

Cranberries on a November evening. My thoughts turn to an unforgettable night one June, exactly twenty years ago. Right here on this narrow track across the mire. I hear the trumpeting of the birds from which they take their name, cranes.

We arrive at Store Mosse late one evening with a longing for all the delights of the warm summer night: the light, the frag-rant smells, the drumming love display of the snipes. Perhaps,

Below: The bugling of whooper swans on the mire at first light is a timeless experience of nature. Above: Wigeon.

"...with a longing for all the delights of the summer night: the light, the fragrant smells, the drumming love display of the snipes," writes Stefan Edman.

When we stop to get a proper bearing on the sound, though, we discover that mingled with it is another, unmistakable kind of music. Accordions! Out here among the bog myrtle and sedge? Yes, we are unlucky enough to have chosen this particular Saturday to come here, when the "mature youth" of the area has descended on Svänö for an evening of old-time dancing. A different kind of "trance" to the one we have come to see.

With the strains of the Koster Waltz ringing in our ears, we retreat to the car and drive to the western side of Store Mosse, to Blådöpet and the orchid-rich Björnekulla Fen. No mean alternative for the nature lover.

Magnificent, gaunt, bathed in light, desolate. An immense inland sea, but on land. An austere wilderness. In winter, wet, frozen, cold and severe. In summer, seething with life, with voices crying out from the carpet of the mire and the whine of billions of starving, expectant mosquito mothers.

It is not without a sense of reverence that you make your way across Store Mosse. Beneath you is a seven metre deep pile of peat, built up over five thousand years from the remains of *Sphagnum* mosses which grew from the sandy bed of an ice age lake known to the scientists as Fornbolmen. For those who are content with the aesthetic merits of the area, the greens, yellows and crimsons of the bog mosses make a magnificent display in the peat landscape.

"Store Mosse deserves a mass in its honour. It could certainly be performed on a summer's day..."

A day on Store Mosse can offer an encounter with Sweden's flesh-eating plants. Sundews and butterwort, which close their leaves hungrily on the flies trapped in their sticky secretions. Or the yellow-flowered greater bladderwort, floating on the pools and moats of the bog, which opens the tiny door in a hundredth of a second to suck an unsuspecting aquatic insect inside of its food bladder.

Or you can wander in search of hobbies and goshawks. Or listen to the anxious, two-note call of the golden plover, in almost mystic harmony with the austere desolation of the mire.

As evening approaches, try walking out to Lövö and Svänö, two islands of glacial till that rise from the bog, to discover a contrast to the wild, sterile, millennia-old peatland: a farmed landscape dating from the nineteenth century. Here there were once herb-rich hay meadows and pastures.

Population growth made it necessary to lower the surfaces of several of the lakes in this mire landscape, where for half a century or more large areas were mown to eke out the hay crops. Today they are becoming overgrown with birch and goat willow. However, under the national park legislation, significant areas are now being managed, with a view to retaining the original mix of natural and cultural landscape.

Store Mosse deserves a mass in its honour. It could certainly be performed on a summer's day. But it could equally be sung on a raw, overcast November evening, when the twilight is beginning to fade and a crow calls out from a stunted, centuries-old pine in this vast, open sea of peat, drooping under the load of ripe cranberries.

with a bit of luck, we may even hear the galloping hooves of the rare jacksnipe high above us.

Whooper swans fly from Lake Kävsjön and Herrestadsvattnet out to the small, grassy pools in the mire to feed. In the 1970s, it was still unusual to see whooper swans breeding in the south of Sweden. Store Mosse, though, was one of the few sites you could rely on, described as early as the beginning of the century by the celebrated zoologist-writer Edvard Wibeck.

The wild cries of the crane always send a prehistoric shiver down my spine. Now, like twenty years ago, up to ten pairs nest on Stora Gungflyet, the mire that was formed when Kävsjön was lowered. I remember my wife and I heading towards Svänö in the hope of catching a glimpse of the remarkable birds through our binoculars.

Despite the poverty of the mire habitat, the red fox manages to find quite a few things to eat.

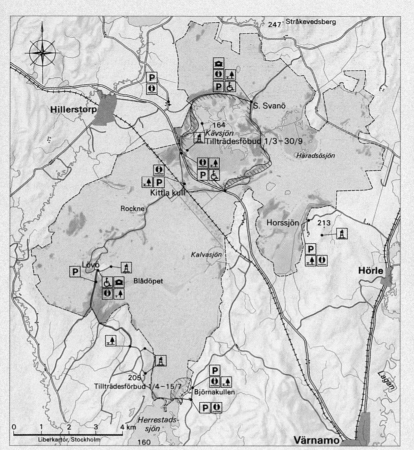

The short-eared owl likes to hunt in open, treeless country.

After congregating for their spring dance, cranes pair off and head for remote bogs to breed. Store Mosse has a sizeable population of the species.

Foundation The national park was established in 1982, in order to preserve the marsh complex in a natural or largely unaltered state. In 1988, Store Mosse National Park was awarded the European Diploma for Nature Conservation.

Location Slightly over ten kilometres northwest of Värnamo in the municipalities of Gnosjö, Vaggeryd and Värnamo, Jönköping County.

Area The total area is 7850 hectares (19,397 acres) of which 7491 hectares are land and 359 hectares water surface. Of the land area, 6692 hectares are marshland, 692 hectares evergreen forest, 65 hectares broad-leaved forest, 20 hectares mixed forest and 22 hectares meadowland.

Attractions The broad marshes. The low sandbanks that wind through the marshes. The birdlife of Lake Kävsjön. The views from Björnakullen and Kvarnberget. The pastoral landscapes of Svanö and Lövö.

Visiting Store Mosse The national park is easy to reach from all directions. There are parking areas and scenic outlooks at Björnakullen and Lake Horssjön. From the main entrance and information centre at Lake Kävsjön there is a path leading to two bird observation towers, one of which is adapted for handicapped persons. The cabins on Svanö and Lövö can be used as occasional overnight sleeping facilities. There are some thirty kilometres of hiking trails in the national park, one around Lake Kävsjön, and another from the Rockne sand formations and across the marshes to Björnakullen.

Marsh helleborine, a pretty species in the genus *Epipactis*, has a preference for calcareous fens.

Sånfjället

Sånfjället is a graceful mountain that rises in lonely majesty above the forest of central Härjedalen. The mountain and the surrounding forest are well-known as among the most important bear habitats in all of Scandinavia. It is also a place of unusually distinct and well-preserved geological formations created by meltwater from the last ice-age glacier.

LANDSCAPE Härjedalen is a highland area with a broad and somewhat desolate landscape. It consists of gently rounded, tree-clad hills, above which rise isolated barren peaks that can be seen from far off. Sånfjället is the highest among them, and its striking profile reaches particularly imposing heights.

"It is strange how the churches here, especially at Hede and Vemdalen, also show a family resemblance to the mountains, in particular to Sonfjället."
KARL-ERIK FORSSLUND (1915)

The slopes of Sånfjället are steep, rising at a steady angle to ca. 800 metres over the surrounding area, and 1278 metres above sea level. Together with seven lower pinnacles, it forms a horseshoe that opens to the south and cradles the deep wilderness valley of Sododalen. Soil is scarce on the massif's higher elevations, which are covered with boulders worked loose by the action of ice. Lichens and the quartzite bedrock impart a light grey colour to the boulders and rock faces.

Perhaps the most interesting natural features are the run-off channels that cover an area of seven square kilometres. The eighty-odd channels, which can be up to twelve metres deep, were formed toward the end of the last ice age when meltwater ran between the edge of the glacier and the side of the mountain. Seen from above, the mountainside looks like a vast field of enormous furrows ploughed by a giant.

Other interesting geological phenomena include the channels formed where meltwater worked its way under the glacier, and the largest complex of prehistoric outwash plains in Sweden.

The slopes of Sånfjället are so even that there are few depressions in which ponds or lakes can form. But there are many small streams, and just inside the eastern boundary runs a sizeable river, the Valmen.

Above: Like the cone of an extinct volcano, the solitary figure of Sånfjället rises above the forests of Härjedalen. Far left: Sånfjället is a stronghold of the brown bear.

VEGETATION Half of the national park is covered in evergreen forest, with isolated trees growing at elevations of up to 1000 metres. Spruce occurs at higher elevations on Sånfjället than anywhere else in Sweden, due to the continental climate with its comparatively high summer temperatures. Most regional varieties of evergreen forest are represented in the park, from dry pine to dense spruce with verdant undergrowth; the latter type, however, is found only at isolated locations along watercourses.

Most of the primarily spruce forest grows on the mountain slopes, whereas pine predominates in dry and level areas such as the outwash plains in Valmen Valley. In the moist ground along the Valmen River, there is a luxuriant growth of tall spruces mixed with great sallow, birch, grey alder and other broad-leaved species. In these woods, there are patches of lush undergrowth of such plants as alpine sowthistle, meadowsweet, wood cranesbill and wild angelica, as well as the lady, narrow buckler and ostrich ferns.

The spruce forest has been left largely undisturbed and has a magnificent primeval appearance, with trees up to 250 years old and numerous decaying trunks on the ground. The pine forest at lower levels, on the other hand, was logged about a century ago, and also shows the effects of forest fire. In the transition zone from the evergreen forest to the barren heights, there is a narrow strip of mountain birch.

Few vascular plants grow on the boulder-strewn barrens at

View from Sånfjället as winter begins to melt into spring.

higher elevations; but there are lichens in abundance, especially reindeer moss, *Cladonia stellaris, Cetraria islandica and crustose lichens.* Lower down on the mountain, several plants have taken hold to form a dry heath of crowberry, heather, alpine bearberry, dwarf birch and thick billowing carpets of lichen. The unusually rich flora of lichens in the park is due to the fact that it is not used for reindeer herding to the same extent as most other parts of the mountains.

ANIMAL LIFE An important motive for Sånfjället's establishment as a national park at the start of the 20th century was to protect the endangered remnant of Sweden's brown bear population. It was believed at the time that only a single bear remained in the area. Several decades later, however, the population had recovered; by the 1940s, Sånfjället and surroundings had become one of the most important bear habitats in all of Scandinavia.

The moose population is well-established in the park, which is also the western limit of the roe deer's range. The wolverine wanders through the park on occasion, and the lynx does so on a more frequent basis. The pine marten, red fox, mountain hare and red squirrel are also present. Typical birds of the barren heights are the ptarmigan, golden plover, meadow pipit and snow bunting. Typical birds of the forest are the redpoll, brambling, chaffinch, mistle thrush, redwing and pied flycatcher. Other inhabitants are the goshawk, capercaillie, and assorted owls and woodpeckers.

THE HUMAN PRESENCE Due to the generally poor soils, human exploitation of the Sånfjället area has always been rather limited, and it retains the look of a pristine wilderness. In former times, it was used primarily for hunting and cattle grazing. There were several summer grazing camps, or shielings, outside the park boundaries; the one at Nyvallen was still in use as recently as 1996.

A goshawk with freshly captured prey.

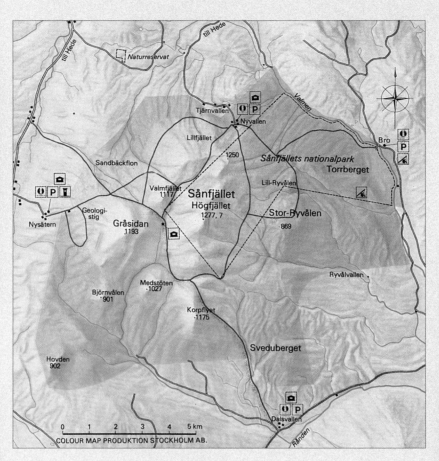

Map labels: till Hede · Naturreservat · till Hede · Valmen · Tjärnvallen · Nyvallen · Bro · Lillfjället · 1250 · Sånfjällets nationalpark · Torrberget · Sandbäckflon · Valmfjället 1117 · Lill-Ryvålen · Sånfjället Högfjället 1277, 7 · Stor-Ryvålen · 869 · Nysätern · Geologi-stig · Gråsidan 1193 · Ryvålvallen · Medstöten ·1027 · Björnvålen ·901 · Korpflyet ·1175 · Sveduberget · Hovden 902 · Dalsvallen · Rånden · 0 1 2 3 4 5 km · COLOUR MAP PRODUKTION STOCKHOLM AB.

Alpine gentian delighted Linnaeus "with the exceptional blue of its flowers".

Spruce cone seeds are the red squirrel's favourite food.

The melancholy fluting of the golden plover cannot escape the mountain walker.

Foundation	The national park was established in 1909, then consisting of 2622 hectares on the mountain's northeast flank; it was expanded to its present size in 1988. The purpose of the park is to preserve a southerly section of Sweden's mountain range, including a forest and a mountain peak, in its natural state.
Location	Approximately fifteen kilometres south of Hede in the Municipality of Härjedalen, Jämtland County.
Area	The national park includes 10,440 hectares (25,797 acres) of dry land and forty hectarcs of water surface. The land area consists of 5750 hectares evergreen forest, 850 hectares mountain birch forest, 2400 hectares mountain heath, 1100 hectares boulders and stone rubble, and 300 hectares marshland.
Attractions	The view from Sånfjället's summit. The glacial run-off channels on the western and southern slopes of Mt. Gråsidan. The primeval spruce forest. The lichen vegetation.
Visiting Sånfjället	It is easy to travel by car to the national park, either to Nyvallen where there is a combined shelter and information facility, or to the Valmen River where there is a parking area and wind-shelter. There are several marked trails which are accessible year round. A good place to enter the park during winter is Nysätern.

Tiveden

Tiveden National Park is a large tract of evergreen forest with deep fissure valleys, chaotic expanses of huge boulders, and a powerful sense of wilderness. Located near the heart of southern Sweden, the park offers the opportunity to experience a fascinating natural setting, and to wander through a beautiful forest landscape of many lakes.

LANDSCAPE Few parts of the country have been so surrounded by legends of outlaws and wilderness as has Tiveden. The stories have their origins in the mystery evoked by the sharply broken landscape, with its gigantic boulders. The area has always been difficult to settle, farm or even traverse. During the Middle Ages, Tiveden forest covered a large part of the area between the two major lakes of Vänern and Vättern, forming a strategic barrier between the ancient regions of Götaland and Svealand. The national park preserves merely one percent of that uninterrupted forest, but testifies nevertheless to the vastness and difficult, dramatic terrain of the former wilderness.

> *"The sullen, bewildering ways of the wastelands wind wildly away; while Tiveden's tangled tussocks and trees cast their silent, stifling spell."*
> ERNFRID TJÖRNE (1943)

Tiveden is part of south-central Sweden's fissure valley landscape. The national park is situated between lakes Unden and Vättern on a horst, a section of ground that was lifted up by movements of the earth's crust some 400–600 million years ago. That same geological process resulted in the formation of the two

Left: **At Stenkälla the visitor encounters the soul of the Tiveden forest.**
Below: **The goldeneye is commonly seen on Tiveden's nutrient-poor lakes.**

lakes' enormous basins, and in a number of large and small fissures in Tiveden's bedrock. The latter contain many huge boulders that have worked free of the bedrock. Two of the most impressive accumulations are at Stenkällebergen and Tärnekullen, where moss-covered blocks of stone up to ten metres high convey the essence of Tiveden.

The national park's highest point is 235 metres above sea level, and roughly 150 metres above the surface of Lake Vättern. From Mt. Lilla Trollkyrka there is an excellent view over Tiveden's forest and the wide blue waters of Lake Vättern in the distance.

During the last ice age, moraine deposits were removed from higher elevations, as a result of which there is a great deal of bare rock on the ridge crests. The beautiful, round, ice-polished rocks give the hills much of their distinctive character. The moraine soils in the fissure valleys are in many places capped by marshes and ponds.

The national park contains some thirty lakes and ponds. The water in some of the lakes is clear from lack of nutrients, whereas most of the ponds are tawny with the colour of nourishing humus. The lakes form clearings in the landscape, providing good views of the rugged terrain. The largest lake, Trehörningen, has a long and inviting sandy beach.

Below: The hazelhen feels at home in a dense forest of spruce, mixed with birch and alder.
Bottom: The northern shore of Stora Trehörningen is known as "White Sand".
Opposite: In the mighty Tiveden forest, man seems very small.

VEGETATION The plant life of the national park reflects the lack of nutrients in its granite bedrock, as well as the thin soils and the special characteristics of the fissure valley landscape. On the ridge heights grow typically uniform stands of tall, dry pines. In the larger valleys, there are mixed woods of pine and spruce, and even a few stands entirely of spruce. Some broad-leaved trees are also present, primarily aspen and birch. Numerous ponds, fens and pine-wooded bogs contribute to the park's pleasing diversity.

"Here, as the whining mosquitoes dance, the scene is haunted by an age that was before man: the flourishing scions of ancient fern forests, and hanging erratic boulders overgrown with moss, piled up into Cyclopean walls."
VERNER VON HEIDENSTAM ("TIVEDEN", 1895)

The flora of Tiveden is very limited, and almost entirely lacking in species that require a good supply of nutrients. On the other hand, species associated with poor soils are quite abundant. These include the rocky heights' thick carpets of reindeer moss which, on the flanks of the ridges, give way to heather and lingonberry. Common flowers of the spruce forest are chickweed wintergreen, twinflower, golden-rod, common cow-wheat and may lily. In the fens of the valley floors grow bog bilberry, bog myrtle, Labrador tea, hare's-tail cotton-grass and dwarf birch, the last-named at its southern limit in Sweden.

The forest of Tiveden has been strongly influenced by two forces: logging conducted from the 18th to the 20th century; and many forest fires, including the great fire of 1835, in the aftermath of which most of today's forest has grown.

Even though the national park's forest has been affected by human activity, it may be assumed that the most difficult terrain has remained relatively undamaged. This is evidenced by the scattered presence of trees up to 300 years old, as well as standing dead trees and fallen trunks.

ANIMAL LIFE The historical continuity of Tiveden's forest is also reflected in certain elements of the park's animal life. An inventory of beetles disclosed a rich variety of no less than 740 species, many of them vulnerable to the modern forestry from which they are spared in Tiveden. Frequently sighted mammals are the moose, roe deer, pine marten, hare, red squirrel and various small rodents

The bird life is typical of sparse evergreen forests, including such species as the coal, willow and crested tits. Woodpeckers and owls benefit from the park's many dead and hollow trees; the presence of the three-toed woodpecker is of particular interest. There are sizeable populations of capercaillie and hazelhen in the forest, and of the goldeneye which nests in most of the lakes. Other species common to the area include the woodpigeon, treecreeper, bullfinch, nightjar, crossbill and parrot crossbill.

THE HUMAN PRESENCE The legends of Tiveden reach far back into history. As early as the 16th century, King Gustav Vasa worried that the area was a hideout for forest bandits. But such legends have little basis in fact: Tiveden was far too desolate and uninviting to offer shelter to human beings.

There has never been any farmhouse or other permanent settlement within the park area. Humans came to the forest at the beginning of the 18th century in order to cut wood for production of the charcoal that was needed for the region's iron industry. This was followed, a bit into the 20th century, by thinning and clearcutting. The traces of all past human activities within the park are gradually being covered over by vegetation.

Above: The raven is a hardy bird that stays on even when the snow begins to fall.
Below: Small pools are a typical feature of the boulder-strewn Tiveden forest.

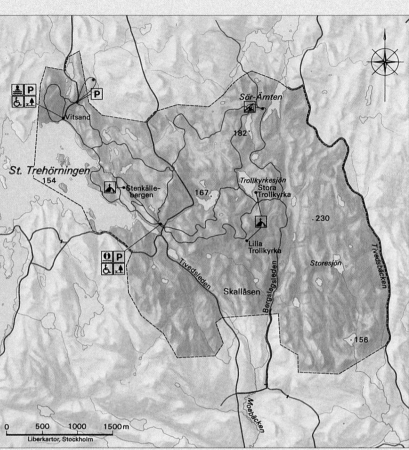

The robin prefers coniferous forests. Its melodious spring song can mainly be heard in the evening and at night.

In the damp hollows between the outcrops of ancient rock, bog mosses spread over logs and boulders.

Tivedstorp, to the north of the national park, is a reminder of how early settlers carved new farmland from difficult terrain. Nowadays the croft is a popular place for a break during a visit to Tiveden.

Foundation	The national park was established in 1983, in order to preserve a large uninterrupted forest in its natural state.
Location	Between lakes Unden and Vättern in the municipalities of Laxå and Karlskoga, Örebro and Skaraborg counties.
Area	The total area of the park is 1353 hectares (3343 acres), of which 1216 hectares are land and 137 water surface. Of the land area, 1153 hectares are evergreen forest, and 200 hectares marshland.
Attractions	The wild and rugged forest landscape. The beautiful forest lakes. The giant boulders at Stenkälla. The view from Stora and Lilla Trollkyrka. The primeval forest at Stenkälla, Tärnekullen and Trollkyrka. The sandy beach at Trehörningen.
Visiting Tiveden	The easiest way to approach the national park is from Highway 49 between Karlsborg and Askersund. A narrow road, Tivedsleden, runs through the area; it passes Stenkällebergen, where there is a parking area and an information display. There are 25 kilometres of hiking trails which pass the most interesting sights.

In exceptional cases, a wood ants' nest can be as tall as a man and house as many inhabitants as Stockholm.

Tresticklan

Along the border with Norway in western Dalsland lies the huge rocky wilderness of Tresticklan. With an area of thirty square kilometres, its the largest uninhabited and roadless tract in southern Sweden. Visitors to the national park are greeted by the sight of pristine forest, beautiful lakes and a remarkable landscape.

LANDSCAPE Along with Tyresta and Tiveden national parks, Tresticklan is located within the fissure valley landscape of southern Sweden. The three parks form lie in a straight line across the breadth of Sweden, and together they provide a representative sample of the fissure valley landscape's natural conditions. But each of the parks also has it own distinguishing features: In Tyresta it is the primeval forest, in Tiveden the rugged terrain of giant boulders, and in Tresticklan the strange protruding shapes of the area's bedrock.

Tresticklan is sometimes described as an area over which a giant has furiously dragged a rake from north to south—a description which evokes the sharply broken terrain's regular pattern of valleys running parallel between narrow, rocky ridges. It is possible to hike north or south along the longest ridges for up to five kilometres with little change in elevation; but travelling east or west means climbing up and down the steep flanks of the ridges. This unique topography continues a ways into Norway.

The parallel ridges are believed to have assumed their present outlines when the softer bedrock between them eroded. In several places, the general north-south pattern is interrupted by fissures running at right angles. This is particularly noticeable near Lake Tresticklan, which extends into several valleys. The lack of mineral soils on the heights is something of a mystery, since the entire area is too elevated to have ever been washed bare by the waves of a sea.

There are some eighty lakes and ponds in the national park . All of them have a naturally low concentration of nutrients, and are therefore vulnerable to the widespread acidification that has affected this part of the country. Previously, the level of Lake Stora Tresticklan has varied widely in connection with the generation of hydroelectric power from the Tresticklan River, outside the park. But since the park's establishment, such variations in the lake's surface level have been limited.

VEGETATION Tresticklan is dominated by evergreen forest that is 100-150 years old, but the ages of some individual specimens exceed 250 years. All indications are that most of the forest has grown from the ashes of an extensive fire in the mid-19th century; natural conditions prevail, with minimal human impact. There has been some logging of individual trees, especially near lakes Stora Tresticklan and Boksjön; and up until the middle of the 20th century, the area was used by nearby farms for limited grazing. But considering its location in Southern Sweden, the forest is on the whole remarkably intact.

The larger part of Tresticklan consists of sparse, open stands of pine. In many places, the rocks are covered with carpets of pastel-coloured lichens. The lichen known as reindeer moss predominates and other lichens of the genuses *Cladonia*, *Cetraria* and *Cornicularia* are also present. In the valleys and hollows, the pine woods are taller and denser, and include elements of aspen, birch and spruce.

Due to the broken terrain, the marshes are many but small—seldom larger than five hectares. Their vegetation includes hare's-

Opposite: Lakes and sparse pine forests on rocky ground are characteristic features of Tresticklan.
Below: Reindeer lichens cover the majority of rock surfaces.

Precambrian ridges and lake-filled valleys reinforce the wilderness character of Tresticklan.

tail cotton-grass, cross-leaved heath, cranberry, sundews, marsh cinquefoil and milk parsley (marsh hog's fennel). In late summer, many of the fens are painted warm yellow by blossoms of bog asphodel.

ANIMAL LIFE The park's animal life is not very diverse, which is typical for this type of forest landscape. Among the large mammals present are the moose, roe deer, mountain hare and red fox. Birds that nest in tree-holes are common, among them the crested tit, the redstart, the great spotted and black woodpeckers, and the golden-eye. Other frequent visitors are the robin, tree pipit, goldcrest, black grouse, capercaillie, hazelhen and nightjar. The common and green sandpipers can often be seen by the lakes and ponds.

THE HUMAN PRESENCE Tresticklan is a border zone on the periphery of human settlements. But the area has been used for grazing, and three small farms were once established.

The grazing was most intense during the 1930s and '40s, when a hundred or so sheep and a few horses were left to roam freely in the forest during the summer. There has been some iron mining in a few places, as well as some quarrying for quartz in connection with glass-making.

An ancient trading route, Halleleden, runs through the area in an east-west direction. It was used mainly by Swedes in settlements east of Tresticklan, as a supply link to the Norwegian town of Halden.

The mires of Tresticklan are home to sundews, whose sticky tentacles trap insects and then digest their prey.

The common sandpiper, one of the world's commonest shorebirds, nests in Tresticklan. "As monotonous as a pagan flute," is how botanist-writer Sten Selander described its call.

Hallåsen

Bodals-viken

Hälle-tjärn

Lilla Tresticklan

Fiskelös

Stens-tjärnet

Gådde-vattnet

Bok-sjön

Grå Mårren

Orshöjden

Skackle-näset

Stora Tresticklan

Skatetjärn

Moltåsen

St. Aborr-tjärnet

St. Pigetjärnet

Mårrefjället

0   1   2 km

Hans Sjögren, Stockholm

The black woodpecker needs a large territory and, as a result, is not very abundant.

The spinning-wheel churr of the nightjar is no longer heard as often as it used to be. As its name suggests, this bird is active at night and rests by day.

Foundation The national park was established in 1996, in order to preserve a fissure valley landscape in a wilderness area with an extensive natural forest that has been little influenced by human activity.

Location About fifteen kilometres northwest of Ed in the Municipality of Dals Ed, Älvsborg County.

Area The total area of the park is 2909 hectares (7188 acres), of which 2722 hectares are land and 187 hectares water surface. Of the land area, 2524 consist of forest, 192 hectares open marshland, and six hectares grassy areas. The adjoining Lundsneset Nature Reserve in Norway contains 2300 hectares, of which 1900 are land and 400 water surface.

Attractions The unusual terrain. The natural forest and beautiful lakes.

Visiting Tresticklan The easiest approach is from the road along the east shore of Lake Stora Lee. A side road about one kilometre north of Rävmarken leads past Rökullehögen Farm to the old croft of Råbocken. This is the only sign-posted road to the park. There is a parking area and information display at Råbocken, from which the Halleleden trail runs for just under a kilometre to the park border. In addition to Halleleden, which continues on into Norway, there are also trails along the shore of Lake Stora Tresticklan and past the old homestead of Bråtane. A side-trail leads up to the park's high point, Orshöjden.

Tyresta

Tyresta National Park is something so remarkable as a large pristine forest just twenty kilometres south of Stockholm's centre. The park provides the opportunity for long walks in a landscape of ancient trees, strongly-scented marshes and beautiful lakes. It is a place where visitors can experience the silence of the primeval forest, with its characteristic plants and animals.

LANDSCAPE The region south of Stockholm is part of the most distinctive fissure valley landscape in Sweden. It is a landform characterised by a regular pattern of tree-clad hills, and hollows filled with lakes or farmland. The hills are quite steep in places; but the vertical rise between the floors of the hollows and the highest hillcrests is seldom more than fifty metres. There is no prominence that could be called a mountain.

The fissure valley landscape is limited to parts of southern Sweden and the southern tip of Finland. It is the weathered remnant of an ancient mountain range that reached its maximum height about two milliard years ago. Subsequent movements in the earth's crust fractured the bedrock, producing a network of large and small fissures. The largest are clearly visible from the air, as narrow valleys that stretch for miles. The smaller fissures can be readily distinguished at ground level.

During the last ice age, the entire Tyresta area was pressed down below sea level. As the ice cap melted away and the land emerged from the sea, stones and soil were washed into the hollows by waves, and the ice-worn rocks lay smooth as those of today's archipelagos. All this took place some 8000 years ago, but the effects continue to influence Tyresta and its vegetation. Among the national park's most distinguishing features are the extensive areas of rocky outcrops, with their lichens and sparse stands of pine. The primeval bedrock consists largely of gneiss and gneiss-granite.

There are nine lakes and ponds within the park boundaries; all lie in fissure valleys and are poor in nutrients. Several of the lakes along the Åva River have been treated with lime since 1976 in order to maintain fish stocks and water quality. Of particular value are the Åva River sea trout, which are used for reproduction and the stocking of other waters.

VEGETATION Tyresta's most interesting natural features are associated with its forest. In the park's western section, there are lovely stands of untouched ancient trees. Many of these stands are 120-350 years old; the oldest pines among them first took root about 400 years ago. Fallen and standing dead trees from still earlier times can be found in rocky areas and along the edges of the

marshland. On the whole, the area has been left in a remarkably natural state that is virtually unique for the entire southern third of Sweden.

Sparse and airy stands of pine dominate the rocky heights, while dense spruce and mixed forest prevail in the hollows. Marshes redolent with the scent of Labrador tea occupy the hollows of the rocky terrain. Deviating from this general pattern is an area of broad-leaved forest east of Lake Årsjön. In 1914, a forest fire raged through 150 hectares of this area and destroyed much of its thin soil. But the forest has slowly recovered, starting with the typical pioneer species of birch and pine.

Opposite: **Two islets seem to hover over Lake Stensjön at dawn, a wilderness scene just twenty kilometres south of Stockholm.**
Below: **The capercaillie is a bird of undisturbed coniferous forests and thrives in Tyresta.**

The hollows between the pine-clad areas of poor, rocky ground have moister soil, where spruces and deciduous trees can also grow.

The ancient forest provides favourable conditions for a number of plants and animals that cannot adapt to the managed forest of today. Despite the Stockholm region's air pollution, the park has an unusual abundance of beard and other arboreal lichens. *Alectoria sarmentosa*, which has sharply declined elsewhere in southern Sweden, is alive and well in Tyresta. Among the most interesting of the park's at least 150 species of bryophytes are the liverwort, green shield-moss *Anastrophyllum* and *Dicranum*.

ANIMAL LIFE Tyresta's animal life is typical for forests of its type. Moose, roe deer, mountain hare, red squirrel, pine marten and red fox inhabit the park. Lynx occasionally wander through the forest, primarily during the winter. Some eighty bird species nest in the park—an unusually high figure for a predominantly evergreen forest. The most prevalent species are the chaffinch and the robin; the goldcrest, jay and various tits are common among the spruces. Also well-represented are the capercaillie, nightjar, goshawk, sparrowhawk, eagle owl, lesser spotted woodpecker, osprey and the park's symbol, the pygmy owl.

THE HUMAN PRESENCE Ancient remains in the Tyresta area indicate that it has been inhabited at least since the Viking Era (ca. 800-1050 A.D.). On the summit of the promontory on Lake Stensjön's north shore is the remnant of a fortress that dates from the Iron Age. The oldest remaining buildings in Tyresta village were built in the mid-1700s, but most of them date from the early 1800s. The village retains most of its character from the agrarian society of the 1800s, and is one of the best-preserved historic settlements in the Stockholm region.

It is not entirely clear how Tyresta has avoided the fate of southern Sweden's other forests, nearly all of which have been logged during the past few centuries. But problems of ownership and timber transport have played a role. A decisive event was the Municipality of Stockholm's acquisition of the forest in 1936, just as it was about to be logged.

ERIKA BJERSTRÖM

Tyresta – a breathing space near the city

Breathing space. A space to breathe in. These days, one of the most endangered of all states of mind.

Sergels Torg in central Stockholm, on a morning in March. Breathing space is hard to come by. A dusty glass column strains skywards, a tree trunk bereft of its crown. The traffic surges round the roundabout, tolerably ornamented with exhaust-resistant evergreens.

Every surface is rectangular. Every structure hard. A pneumatic drill hammers away, and people hurry past. The windows of the Cultural Centre stare unseeing over the heart of the city. Little space to breathe, and a struggle for space to live.

Twenty kilometres away, beyond the temporarily deserted apartment blocks of the suburbs, are the soaring columns of ancient pines. Here there is only the silence to disturb you. First nothing, and then a faint rushing noise. Urban man pricks up his ears. It sounds like a commuter train, but it is the soughing of the pines. A native sound that does not come barging in on our human senses, but waits to be invited. And suddenly it is there. Space to breathe. Breathing space.

Tyresta's virgin forest is the breathing space of the big city, physically and above all spiritually. This particular day is the first day of spring. A great tit, drunk with the bright March

Below: Many of Tyresta's pine trees have reached an age of two or three hundred years, some even four hundred. Above: Hepatica.

light, is hoping to attract a female; a willow tit sings as if trying to defy both the laws of physics and its body weight of just three grams; the snow is melting on the south-facing slopes; and the cowberry plants are a defiant shiny green, the cruel winter now forgotten.

Patterns and shapes surpass one another: the aged pine that has lost its bark, to reveal the smooth, defenceless velvet beneath; a younger, healthier relative, whose red bark gleams with overweening pride.

Below the ground you can sense the muffled resonance of ore, and the smooth outcrops still remember the waves of the Baltic which once reigned over this landscape. But sea and islands made way for virgin forest, a bare, uncovered forest landscape of a unique kind.

Now the sea is a day's walk away, a walk that takes you through a remarkable fractured landscape, which came into being when the mountain range was twisted and cracked at the beginning of time, an inconceivable 600 million years ago. The ice age came and froze the sea. In the valleys, the life-giving earth survived, but on the many hilltops it is eggshell-thin. This was where the great mass of ice advanced.

The forest has many rooms to display: its own open-air sculpture museum, a plateau where old trees have fossilized into statues that stand out effectively against the sky; or the banqueting hall, where the cone-studded spruce tops hang like sunlit chandeliers beneath the forest ceiling, high above the floor of grey boulders and fire-singed stumps.

On bare expanses of rock, the trees suddenly become corpulent and grow widthways, to make the most of the little nutrition that is to be had. It is as if, out of respect for their more imposing relatives down in the valley, they are taking care not to grow above their heads. In Tyresta's virgin forest, all the trees seem equally tall. They are each other's windbreaks.

But forest and city have some features in common. As in Sergels Torg, a struggle for living space is constantly in progress. An aspen has lost its battle with a pine and grown an extravagant crown, but only in one direction. The two trunks stand side-by-side. A small pine tree has lost its original crown, and a branch, seizing its evolutionary chance, has turned itself into a new one and is now heading for the forest canopy.

On the ground are fallen timbers, relics that now rest in peace, their sap long since dry. Their cavities have been taken over by *Prionus depsarium* and *Nothorhina punctata* – rare and endangered beetles whose existence depends on dead wood.

The white-tailed eagle, high above them, is the master of the forest he surveys. Resting on a current of air, he can see all the way to the rotating clock of the NK department store.

But the city stretches out its claws towards Tyresta, jealous of its monumental independence. It almost manages to reach past the seventies housing of the nearby suburbs to seize hold of these ancient woods. But once those functional structures have disappeared behind a curtain of trees, Tyresta village, with its roots in the Iron Age, emerges to maintain the front against urban modernity.

Luminous moss, fungi such as *Phellinus ferrugineofuscus* and *Phlebia centrifuga*. Viviparous lizard, perch, ruffe, eel and bleak. Pine marten, elk, mink and lynx. Capercaillie, Tengmalm's owl, hawk, tawny and pygmy owl.

Their existence is a triumph. Their primeval home, a victory for the stubborn struggle that has secured the protection of Tyresta's forests. At the entrance to Tyresta, the Environmental Protection Agency proclaims its victory with a large sign announcing in proud letters that this is a national park.

There are thousands of parking spaces, as if there had to be room for the crowds of ice hockey fans that flock to the Globe Arena for a world championship final. Visitors extol the area for its wealth of variation: pastures, lush valleys, mire pools fringed with cloudberries, smooth outcrops of rock, oak woods and dark coniferous forest. The greatest miracle of all is the fact that 400-year-old pines have survived here, despite centuries of farming and forestry. The farmers only felled trees in the immediate vicinity of the village; the remaining areas were left uncultivated and served as pasture for their livestock.

"The city stretches out its claws towards Tyresta, jealous of its monumental independence."

At the beginning of the twentieth century, Tyresta was owned by Emma Sofia Dahlgren, and, unlike her neighbours, she refused to sell the right to the timber. Finally, in the 1930s, Ivar Kreuger bought the forest with a view to felling it, but then the politicians stepped in and displayed something they get no thanks for today – far-sightedness. In 1936, Tyresta was protected. Sweden's nature conservation movement was endowed with a fragment of living natural history, for national parks like Tyresta and Tiveden also have the onerous duty of providing a home for memories. They remind their visitors of all the virgin forests that have been destroyed by the same forces as built the concrete jungles of the cities.

Back in Sergels Torg on a March afternoon. The same bright light, but no jubilant willow tits. The neon lights are coming on. There is no silence to disturb you, only a noisy barrage of impatience and things on the move. In the fading daylight beyond the railway bridge you can just make out the silhouette of Stockholm's City Hall, and another breathing space comes to mind. Even a city can have its breathing spaces, in this case the recollection that the water passing through the capital is clean enough to swim in.

And suddenly there is a bond between Tyresta and the waterways of Stockholm.

Stockholmers very rarely think of going down to the City Hall for a swim. And it isn't every day they travel out to Tyresta to visit its virgin forest.

But the mere knowledge that they can, that the possibility exists, instils a quiet sense of exultation.

Breathing space.

Ancient, massive pines in the national park.

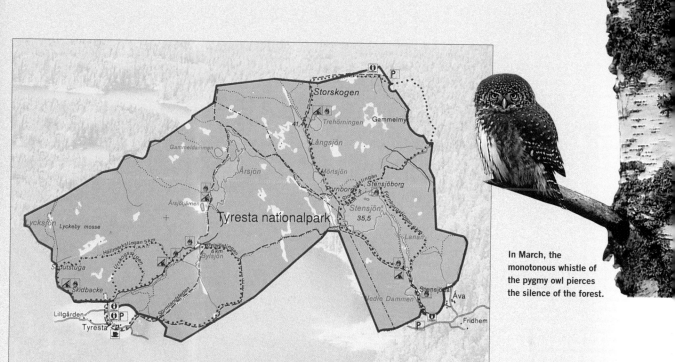

In March, the monotonous whistle of the pygmy owl pierces the silence of the forest.

Tyresta's proximity to Stockholm makes it an attractive forest area for outdoor recreation.

Near the entrance to Tyresta is the Environmental Protection Agency's National Parks Centre, shaped like a rough-hewn map of Sweden.

Foundation The national park was established in 1993, in order to preserve a representative fissure valley landscape with extensive primeval forest and other valuable natural features. Adjoining the national park is the Tyresta Nature Reserve which was established in 1986, and expanded in 1993 in connection with the national park's establishment. The nature reserve and national park are managed by the Tyresta Forest Foundation, formed jointly by the Swedish Environmental Protection Agency, the Stockholm County Administrative Board, and the municipalities of Stockholm, Haninge and Tyresö.

Location Twenty kilometres south of Stockholm in the municipalities of Tyresö and Haninge, Stockholm County.

Area The total area of the park is 1970 hectares (4868 acres), of which 1880 hectares are land and ninety hectares lake surface. Of the land area, 1816 hectares are forest, 62 hectares open marshes, and two hectares meadowland. The adjoining nature reserve contains 2730 hectares, of which 2400 are land and 330 waters of the Baltic Sea. The combined forest area of the national park and the nature reserve is 3916 hectares (9676 acres).

Attractions The primeval forest near the village of Tyresta. The "Urskogsslingan" nature trail which begins at the information centre. The view from and the ancient fortress on the hill near Lake Stensjön. The wilderness atmosphere by the beautiful Lake Årsjön. Tyresta village, with its information facilities and the National Parks Centre.

Visiting Tyresta The main entrance to the national park is located near the village of Tyresta, which can be easily reached by bus or private car. The National Parks Centre, displaying information on the entire park system, was formally opened in June of 1997. The village, which is an interesting attraction in itself, includes an outdoor information display on Tyresta National Park, dining facilities, and the park supervisor's office.

By means of the fifty kilometres of trails running through the park and an adjoining nature reserve, visitors may experience the extensive ancient forest, the lakes with their impressive shoreline cliffs, or stroll all the way to the Baltic Sea.

Töfsingdalen

Töfsingdalen is a wild and remote valley in the mountains of northern Dalarna which includes an interesting assortment of landscapes—dry and inhospitable domains of huge boulders, dense stands of ancient pines, verdant flower-carpeted woods of spruce, small peaceful lakes and rushing waters.

LANDSCAPE The Dalarna massif is characterised by gently rounded smaller mountains that are widely scattered and surrounded by broad, level tracts of evergreen forest. Mt. Långfjället, on the other hand, is part of a large and roadless mountain region that runs westward to Härjedalen and on into Norway. Here, somewhat hidden in a remote valley, lies Töfsingdalen National Park.

"A human being scrambles among these rocks like an ant in a slag heap, unable to get any real grasp of the landscape, since the largest boulders, which are several metres high and which might have provided a viewpoint, are often impossible to climb."

SVEN A. MELLQVIST

The park consists of small lateral valley running north from the Storå River near Mt. Långfjället, along with the ridges on either side, Olåsen and Hovden. The latter reaches a height of 892 metres above sea level. Olåsen means "ridge of stones", a highly appropriate name. Most of the park is covered by large boulders which make it one of the wildest and most inaccessible areas in the southern mountains of Sweden.

The moraines and boulders of Töfsingdalen were left behind when the last ice glacier melted away from the mountains. On the west slope of Olåsen, the moraine runs down to the Storån River in a series of parallel ridges up to twenty metres high. At the base of Olåsen, the descending moraine has dammed up the Storån River at seven places, creating a glittering stairway of small lakes.

VEGETATION Due to park's continental climate and poor soils, its vegetation is dominated by sparse stands of relatively short pines that grow on the mountain slopes. There are also some lovely stands of large pines, including many silvery snags, especially on the slopes of Hovden. An interesting species of the pine forest is the yellow-coloured wolf lichen. It is characteristic of this mountain region, and grows widely on the dead trees of the national park. In areas with the heaviest accumulation of boulders, it is difficult even for pines to take root—apart from a few specimens scattered here and there, along with the odd gnarled birch.

On the damp ground along the Töfsingån River grows a completely different kind of forest—ancient spruces mixed with broad-leaved species which, in an otherwise arid landscape, form a lush oasis on the narrow floor of the valley. Birch, rowan and great sallow provide an element of variation amongst the lofty spruces. Grasses, tall flowering plants, ferns and bird cherry combine to form a ground cover like that of a shady broad-leaved grove.

Among the more common plants are garden angelica, meadowsweet, red campion, wood cranesbill, ostrich fern and lady fern.

Opposite: A dead tree stands sculpture-like on the slopes of Hovden. In the background, Storvätteshågna. Below: Wood cranesbill is one species that flourishes in the herb-rich valley. According to Linnaeus, "no plant is more plentiful in the forests or fairer on the lower mountains".

Wolf lichen has a limited range, mainly occurring in southern Norrland and Värmland. It thrives on the decaying pine stumps of Töfsingdalen. The lichen used to be mixed with meat to poison wolves, hence the name.

Above: In the Töfsingån valley, the spruce forest is dense, and the fertile soil
supports a lush growth of grasses and herbs that is in complete contrast to the bare,
boulder-strewn mountainsides nearby (below).

Such orchids as the lesser twayblade and frog orchid can be discovered here, as well as such hungry plants as baneberry, whorled Solomon's seal, lily of the valley and the large white buttercup. Similar stands of luxuriant forest also grow along the Storån River.

ANIMAL LIFE Moose graze regularly in Töfsingdalen's spruce forest, and beavers have occupied its waters for quite some time. Wolverines and bears wander through the park on occasion, but are not regular visitors. The characteristic bird of the boulder-covered terrain is the wheatear; other common species are the willow warbler, redstart and redwing. The wren, treecreeper, three-toed woodpecker and dipper can also be observed in the park, as can the goosander (common merganser) which nests in dead trees near the Storån River's chain of small lakes.

THE HUMAN PRESENCE Töfsingdalen national park is a pristine wilderness area, with no trace of human settlement, and is included in the Idre Saami Village's summer grazing grounds.

A dipper resting on a rock midstream. It forages on the riverbed, swimming into the current with its head bent low so that the flowing water presses it down.

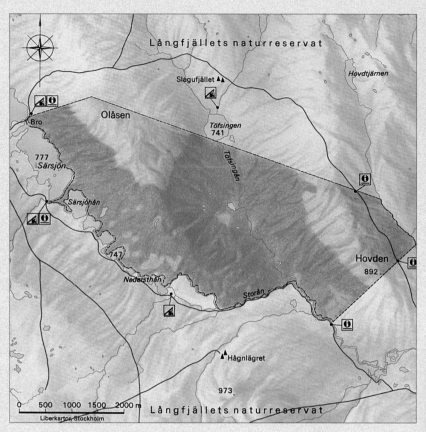

The three-toed woodpecker works its way round tree trunks in search of food, leaving the "ringbarking" marks typical of the species.

Ferns on the lush banks of the Töfsingån.

Baneberry is one of the few members of the buttercup family to produce berries. Its roots were once used as a remedy for acute gout and toothache.

The rocky terrain of Töfsingdalen suits the wheatear better than any other bird, and its spirited behaviour livens up the mountain landscape.

Foundation	The national park was established in 1930, in order to preserve an area of evergreen forest and boulder-strewn terrain in the southern Swedish mountains.
Location	Ca. 35 kilometres north of Idre in the Municipality of Älvdalen, Dalarna County.
Area	The national park contains 1615 hectares (3990 acres), of which two hectares are water surface. Of the land area, 994 hectares are evergreen forest, 170 hectares mixed forest, 260 hectares mountain birch forest, 173 hectares alpine heath and 16 hectares marshland.
Attractions	Large areas of massive boulders. Beautiful ancient pine forest. The view from Hovden ridge. The lush vegetation along the Töfsingån River.
Visiting Töfsingdalen	There are no tourist facilities of any kind in Töfsingdalen, and its terrain is very difficult due to the sea of boulders. There is a rather poor road from the southeast to the Storån River and Siljanskojan, where limited sleeping facilities are available. From there, it is a seven-kilometre hike to the park boundary. An alternative is to walk the twelve kilometres from the Lake Grövelsjön research station to the west.

Vadvetjåkka

Vadvetjåkka, the northernmost national park in Sweden, is located in a little corner of a remote and desolate mountain region northwest of Lake Torneträsk. Apart from the local Saami population, the park is normally visited only by the occasional mountain wanderer who wishes to experience the profound solitude, the rich plant life, or the network of deep caves.

LANDSCAPE The Vadvetjåkka Massif forms a section of the comparatively low mountain landscape north of Torneträsk Valley. The park's unusual character is a result of its open exposure to the moist Atlantic winds that release heavy precipitation over the area. There is a striking difference in climate between Vadvetjåkka and Abisko National Park, a mere two miles distant. Whereas Abisko Valley lies in a rain shadow and is famous for its sunny weather, summers in Vadvetjåkka are full of rain clouds and gloomy skies; in many places, remnants of the deep winter snows linger throughout the summer. But the landscape assumes a special lustre when the clouds suddenly part and brightly illuminate the mountains with their damp heaths and birch forest.

Vadvetjåkka National Park consists largely of a rounded mountain ridge that stretches for six kilometres in a north-south direction. The ridge divides two deep and narrow valleys, reaching its highest point of 1246 metres near the Norwegian border. In the opposite direction, it ends in a crown of 1115 metres from which a steep southern slope descends to a broad valley. The section of lowland included in the park is a beautiful delta with a mosaic of streams, lagoons, marshes and small lakes.

The most common rocks in the park are mica schists which often contain granite, but there is also a thick vein of limestone running along the ridge. The limestone's fertile contribution to the park's vegetation is particularly evident on the southern slope of the ridge. In the park's northern section is a deep cave formed through limestone weathering; at 700 metres long and 140 metres deep, it is the deepest cave yet discovered in Sweden.

VEGETATION The vegetation of the national park is of geographical interest due to its location in the northwestern mountains, which are exposed to winds from the Atlantic. Roughly 300 vascular plants have been discovered here, including such rarities as *Braya linearis*, northern moonwort, northern milk-vetch and mountain sandwort. The greatest species diversity is to be found on the ridge's southern slope, where the limestone bedrock has given rise to a luxuriant birch wood with a ground cover of mountain avens, purple saxifrage, rock speedwell and Scandinavian primrose, as well as large

Opposite: The mouth of Vadvejåkka Stream, where it enters the River Njuoraätno.
Above: One of the pleasures of the mountains is the melodious, almost round-the-clock warbling of the fearless bluethroat in the birchwoods. Below: The Lapland bunting is another characteristic bird of the Scandinavian mountains.

Left: The Cunujåkka Stream, flowing alongside Mount Vadvetjåkka, discharges onto a delta further south, where the pintail (above) and many other birds nest.

quantities of ostrich, male and other ferns.

The birch forest, which takes up a fairly small portion of the park's area, has been damaged by the avalanches that are common here due to heavy accumulations of snow. Alpine heaths account for eighty percent of the park's area, while marshland takes second place. There are fens on the ridge slopes, and large open marshes in the delta.

ANIMAL LIFE The Vadvetjåkka delta abounds with ducks and wading birds, including the teal, scaup, wigeon, pintail, redshank, Temminck's stint, greenshank and red-necked, or northern, phalarope. The bluethroat and the ring ouzel are unusually numerous on the southern slope of the ridge, where many other small birds of the mountain birch forest are also present. On the barren alpine heaths nest the ptarmigan, dotterel and snow bunting. Moose are often seen in the park, and Arctic foxes on occasion.

THE HUMAN PRESENCE Vadvetjåkka is included in the Talma Saami Village's summer grazing lands, and the area is also grazed by reindeer belonging to Saami in neighbouring Norway. Ancient Saami trails to the Norwegian coast pass through the park. For a time, during 1850-1880, this remote area was occupied by a Saami family. Hay has been gathered from the bog-meadows of the delta, and the vegetation still shows traces of human activity.

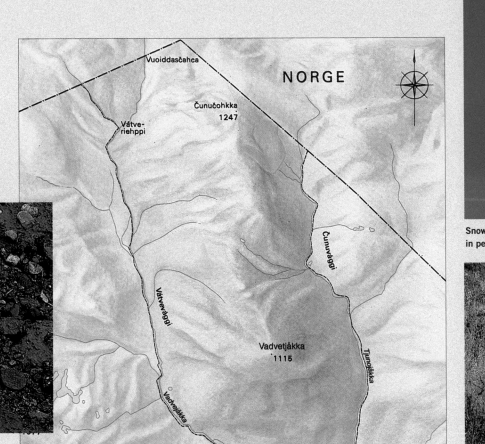

Snowy owl numbers increase
in peak lemming years.

Wet ground with moss in the
southern part of the park.

"One of the fairest ornaments of the
mountains" was how one 19th century
botanist described purple saxifrage.
Its flowers are large in proportion to the
rest of the plant, and it grows in very
barren terrain.

Scandinavian primrose *Primula scandinavica*.

Foundation	The national park was established in 1920, in order to preserve a northern Scandinavian alpine landscape in its natural state.
Location	Northwest of Lake Torneträsk along the border with Norway in the Municipality of Kiruna, Norrbotten County.
Area	The national park contains 2630 hectares (6500 acres), of which 2582 hectares are land and 48 hectares water surface. Of the land area, 2122 hectares consist of alpine heaths, 160 hectares mountain birch forest, 256 hectares marshland and 44 hectares glacier.
Attractions	The vegetation of the ridge's southern slope. The delta with its bird life. The caves.
Visiting Vadvetjåkka	The national park is not easily accessible. One approach is to travel by boat to the north shore of Lake Torneträsk, and from there hike six kilometres to the park boundary. An easier alternative is to hike the twelve kilometres of a marked trail from the train-stop at Låktajåkka. There are no lodging or other facilities within the park.

Ängsö

Ängsö Island is an unusual national park, preserving as it does a genuine 19th-century agricultural landscape. Apart from its significance as a cultural and historical monument to a bygone farming era, the park offers a very pleasing island landscape, with all the floral splendour for which the archipelago north of Stockholm is renowned.

LANDSCAPE The Stockholm Archipelago is usually divided into three zones. The outer zone is characterised by broad expanses of water, clusters of small islands with broad-leaved woods, and bare rocks and skerries. The intermediate zone contains larger islands with evergreen forest, together with clusters of smaller islands and skerries. The inner archipelago consists for the most part of large wooded islands separated by comparatively narrow channels. Ängsö is a relatively small island near the mainland, with many of the inner archipelago's natural and historical features.

The highest point of Ängsö Island is just over 25 metres above sea level, and it is generally quite flat. Most of the bedrock of gneiss and granite is covered by moraine soils and clay. As recently as the 17th century, a narrow channel divided the present island into two separate and nearly equal entities. It was not until the 18th century that the archipelago's land mass had risen sufficiently to make a single island of the divided parts.

Below: Ängsö's wooded meadows, traditional fences and spectacular spring flowers are a delight to behold.
Opposite: Spring on Ängsö is famous for its cowslips, which according to Palmberg's herbal "relieve toothache *ad miraculum*".

VEGETATION The national park has been fundamentally altered by the toil of farmers. Included in the park's management is preservation of the traditional agricultural landscape. But when it was established in 1909, botanists misinterpreted the origins of the flowery meadows and prescribed that they should be left to develop without interference. This led to rapid overgrowth by indigenous species, and a resulting threat to the agricultural features which the park had been established to preserve.

Today, significant portions of the old pastures and meadows are again being maintained by traditional methods. Leaf-fodder is collected from the trees, and a few fields are being farmed. The results can be witnessed during early spring, when thick carpets of wood anemone, hepatica and cowslip cover the ground. Spring pea,

lungwort and lily of the valley also grow in large quantities, as do the marsh marigolds which colour the damp meadows gold. During the summer blossom the wood cranesbill and the cow-wheat *Melampyrum nemorosum*, along with large numbers of elder-flowered lesser butterfly and early marsh orchids.

One-sixth of the island's surface is covered by open meadows, and another sixth by the oak-wooded meadows in the centre of the park. Bordering the open areas are lush groves of oak, ash, lime, aspen and birch. Stands of alder grow along the beaches and in the damp meadows. Most of the broad-leaved woods have established themselves on former meadowland, thus reclaiming what humans once converted to farmland. Some of the broad-leaved groves will be restored to meadows and pastures, while others

> *"Its floral beauty, its stamp of authenticity and palpable atmosphere, its gentle amiability and simple prettiness, all of these things had constantly been recreated by the labour and care of each new year."*
> PROFESSOR LARS-GUNNAR ROMELL (1961)

will be preserved with their flora of woodruff, ramsons, coralroot bittercress and other shade-tolerant plants.

More than half of Ängsö Island is covered in evergreen forest which partially encloses the central meadows. The eastern part of the island has been left completely undisturbed for nearly a century, and now has the appearance of primeval forest. Spruce is the dominant species, but there are also some stands of pine on rocky terrain. Part of the evergreen forest on the west side of the island is being logged in the manner of yesteryear's farmers. All evergreen forest on Ängsö Island is included in the summer grazing area.

ANIMAL LIFE Roe deer and hares are the principal mammals that can be seen on a visit to the island. Ängsö's mixture of natural and agricultural landscape provides excellent conditions for a diverse bird life. The many nest-hole trees are useful to such species as the lesser spotted woodpecker, stock dove, nuthatch and pied flycatcher.

Other common birds are the redstart, redwing, blackcap, goldcrest, treecreeper, garden warbler and thrush nightingale. Buzzards and ospreys nest in the ancient evergreen forest; and in Hemviken cove there is a colony of great crested grebes. Over 75 bird species have been known to nest on the island.

THE HUMAN PRESENCE The first croft was established on the island's southern tip, Hemudden. The crofter made use of existing pastures and hay-meadows, and broke new ground near his cottage. Areas that are today covered in dense evergreen forest were, toward the end of the 18th century, almost completely open as a result of grazing and of logging for lumber and firewood.

The original crofter's cottage from the 1700s was torn down at the beginning of the 19th century and replaced with new buildings. Some of them, including a barn, remain standing; but the old house was replaced in 1954 with a new dwelling for the park supervisor.

The first croft at Hemudden point was built in 1725. There are still farm buildings here, including a cowshed, together with the warden's house.

G.T. Brusewitz

GUNNAR BRUSEWITZ

Ängsö – a foretaste of paradise

Surely, living on Ängsö—a "meadow island" in the archipelago—must be a foretaste of paradise. That is the thought that crosses my mind when Björn Sjöholm, Ängsö's warden, comes to pick me up from Bergshamra and we head east across the sounds of the inner archipelago towards the national park.

It is a fine October day, and the sky is cloud-free and hazy blue above the sea. On some of the islands we pass there are still the fading embers of autumn colours, and in their bays and inlets velvet scoters, goldeneyes, tufted ducks, goosanders and eiders await the signal to depart for the south.

The western shore of Ängsö is dark and sullen as we approach. I remember how disappointed I was the first time I came here, one day in May thirty years ago, expecting to find the Isle of the Blessed, ablaze with orchids, but instead coming face to face with this unwelcoming wall of dark spruce forest.

But all this changes, as if by magic, as we round the southern point and Björn kills the engine to let his boat slip silently in towards the jetty below the croft. Suddenly, an archaic landscape comes into view which seems to have changed little since the days when August Strindberg wrote affectionately about the archipelago at the end of the nineteenth century.

Enclosed pastures with a scattering of oaks and an undergrowth of hazels and junipers, alternating with sunny meadows, open their arms to greet the visitor. Beyond the pastures, dark coniferous forests stretch in three directions, a warming shelter from the wind. The croft and the warden's house are higher up the slope, the old cottage nestling among the hummocks like a Red Leghorn hen, with outhouses of varying sizes and functions flocking round her like chickens.

This is a settlement with traditions going back to 1725, when the first Ängsö crofter, Erik Hansson, moved into the newly built cottage. At that time, Ängsö was still divided into two halves—East and West Island—by a strait which cut diagonally across it, and which eventually was left high and dry by postglacial uplift. Just over a century later, this channel had become a water meadow, which to this day remains a living memorial to the days when the people of the archipelago could sail between the two islands.

"The soft grass of the meadow, like the clear water of the spring, is one of the fundamental joys of human life."

Even as early as the seventeenth century, however, parties of haymakers would row out on light summer nights to the then uninhabited "meadow islands" to mow the grass at dawn, when it was still grey with dew.

Meadows were a concept even in Old Testament days, a divine gift in the same way as the Garden of Eden. They are mentioned in the Book of Psalms: "The meadows are covered with flocks... they shout for joy and sing." The soft grass of the meadow, like the clear water of the spring, is one of the fundamental joys of human life. Indeed, one Linnaean described the mowing of meadows as "the raw material of our earthly happiness". A foretaste of paradise.

In 1914, the last crofter, Carl Edvard Carlsson, was still living at Hemudden point. Carlsson's ecological intuition told him that if the meadows were not mown, they would soon disappear, but how could he challenge the received wisdom of the men of learning? The Royal Academy of Sciences had been entrusted with the management of the new Ängsö National Park and he had been allowed to stay on, provided he undertook to leave the meadows unmown and ungrazed.

At the beginning of the century, the view was that the park-like wooded meadow landscape could only be saved by protecting it from any human interference: man was the exploiter and

Below: **The roe deer requires a very varied diet, so Ängsö's diversity of habitats makes it an ideal place for this species. Above: Elder-flowered orchid.**

destroyer. No one realized that without farmers and their live-stock there would have been no meadows and pastures in the first place. Science seemed to have forgotten the old adage that "meadow is the mother of arable". The first three decades of the national park's existence were therefore a time of humiliation for most of the island. In 1927, the crofter gave up.

Ten years later, towards the end of the 1930s, at least four hectares of once regularly mown meadowland had become overgrown. All the sunny, flower-filled meadows were hidden beneath tree-high shrubs and saplings, or succumbing to the advancing menace of a "dense blanket of alder thickets and alder woods".

A young plant ecologist called Lars-Gunnar Romell was the first to sound the alarm. And years later, in 1961, he again observed, not without irony, that it was "very difficult for the combined forces of an academy and a public authority to replace a single old-fashioned crofter". Romell was worried about the future: "In reality, the challenge is to replace extinct knowledge and ambitions, and an extinct breed of people."

But the kind of people who are prepared to put time and loving care into looking after Ängsö in a traditional way, and who have the necessary insight to do so, are not altogether extinct. Björn Sjöholm and his Fårö-born wife Edit love their job and have managed to combine fence-building, *fägning*—the traditional practice of clearing dead branches and leaves from wooded meadows—haymaking and other old-fashioned occupations with a mobile phone, a forest tractor, a microwave and the other conveniences of the modern age.

They have three cows, plus another ten that are brought here to graze in the summer, six sheep, a number of ducks, turkeys and hens, and a huge watchdog, which all do their bit to create a living smallholding like that of centuries past. This is now the Environmental Protection Agency's official aim for Ängsö, and they have found the right person to serve as its steward.

Down by the point, Björn is burning old branches, and the smoke forms attractive layers in the still air between the birches and ashes and drifts north across the oak-covered pasture, where fence-making is in progress. A chocolate-brown, pearl-studded nutcracker, flying low on ponderous wings, lands on a mossy stump and immediately attacks a hazelnut with her powerful beak.

Björn is recreating the old haymaking island; he knows every pollard and every stump, and understands how the foliage has to be thinned to let in just the right amount of light and give the right "fertilizing hazel shade" about which Linnaeus waxed so lyrical.

At Norrudden, we stop on the meadow by the shore and my thoughts go back to that day in May thirty years ago when it was full of elder-flowered orchids—or "Adam and Eve", to use the plant's evocative Swedish name. Then we follow the walkway across the meadow into Norrskogen, reminiscent of a virgin forest with its tall pines and windthrows. In the far north of

The majestic white-tailed eagle can suddenly appear in low flight above the treetops of Ängsö.

the island, in Svartviken on the edge of Adamsskogen—"Adam's Forest"—we come to a clearing where there are traces of human habitation. We find the remains of a solidly built, semi-underground storehouse, and near it "Adam's Apple Tree" is still growing—another fitting name in paradise.

On the slopes of Stenbacken, beautiful, knobbly pollard limes recall the days when the trees here provided leaves for winter fodder. A sunny pasture, with mossy boulders scattered among trees in autumn splendour. I think of my first visit to Ängsö, when I followed the path along Långängen and saw anemones and cowslips gleaming like a knotted-pile rug beneath the swelling buds of the oaks.

The blues, whites and yellows of Stenbacken set off the lilac-pink bands of bird's-eye primrose in the wetter terrain of Stormaren. On the meadow by Norrudden, there were dense bouquets of elder-flowered orchid, and at the edge of Västerskogen the fragrance of lesser butterfly orchid wafted towards me.

To preserve a piece of ancient farmland, you need someone to farm it, someone who understands how man and nature can interact. What you need is a crofter with a sense of reverence. As I stand by the croft this October day and watch a fence being built, smell the bonfire down by the point, and see the wind fanning the fishing nets hanging up to dry, I feel calm and confident.

Ängsö is finally in good hands. After many anxious years.

Coralroot bittercress grows in shady groves. It gets its Swedish name, "toothroot", from the scales on its rhizomes, which resemble extracted teeth.

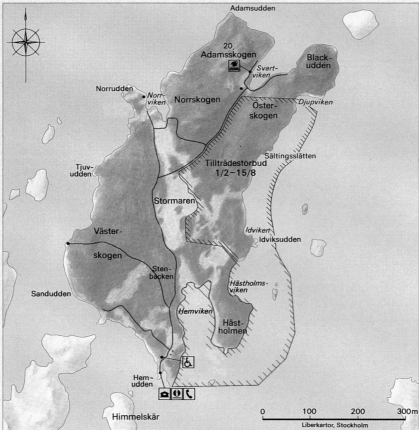

Adamsudden

20. Adamsskogen

Black-udden

Svart-viken

Norrudden

Norr-viken

Norrskogen

Öster-skogen

Djupviken

Sältingsslätten

Tjuv-udden

Tillträdestörbud 1/2 – 15/8

Stormaren

Väster-skogen

Idviken

Idviksudden

Sten-bäcken

Hästholms-viken

Sandudden

Hemviken

Häst-holmen

Hem-udden

Himmelskär

0   100   200   300m

Liberkartor, Stockholm

Apart from elder-flowered orchid, early marsh and several other orchids can be found on Ängsö.

Hemudden from the water.

A colony of great crested grebes has nested in the reeds of Hemviken Bay for many years.

Foundation	The national park was established in 1909, in order to preserve an older agricultural landscape in an essentially unaltered state.
Location	About 2.5 kilometres south of Norrtälje, Stockholm County.
Area	The national park includes 190 hectares (470 acres), of which 73 hectares are land. Of the land area, 38 hectares are evergreen forest, eight hectares broad-leaved forest, twelve hectares wooded meadows, eight hectares meadowland, two hectares cropland, and five hectares shoreline meadows and reed beds.
Attractions	The traditional agricultural landscape. The spring flowers.
Visiting Ängsö	There are fine natural harbours at Svartviken and Norrviken on the northern shore; boats may also dock at a wharf on Hemudden, the southern tip of the island. Near the wharf is a nature centre with information displays. The island's paths are easy to walk, and guided tours can be arranged through the park supervisor. For the protection of birds during the sensitive nesting season, Hemviken and part of the east woods are off-limits from February 1–August 15 every year.

About the authors

GERDA ANTTI – Literary author, born in Tornedalen on the Swedish-Finnish border, now living in Östergötland. Appreciated for her down-to-earth way of writing about people and the natural environment in which they live. Has published some ten novels and collections of short stories since 1961, including *Inte värre än vanligt* ("No worse than usual", 1977), *Jag reder mig nog* ("I'll get by", 1983) and *Bara lite roligt* ("Just a bit of fun", 1994).

ERIKA BJERSTRÖM – Journalist with the environment as her specialized field. Has worked for the Swedish Green Party's periodical *Alternativet*, the national daily *Dagens Nyheter* and the television news programme *Aktuellt*. Selected articles has been put together into the book *Miljövår*. Moderator at seminars.

ANDERS BJÄRVALL – Holds a Ph.D. in zoology, and has for many years been the Swedish Environmental Protection Agency's expert on predatory mammals. A familiar face from television programmes on wolves and other predators, hunting and wildlife conservation. Has written popular science and debate articles in many magazines and books. He is the author of a book on Europe's mammals and co-author of another on reindeer and predators.

GUNNAR BRUSEWITZ – Celebrated artist specializing in watercolours of wildlife and the countryside, and also a productive writer, with a particular preference for bird habitats and Swedish cultural history. Has illustrated some 300 books and written 50 himself, among them the popular *Wings and Seasons* (1980). Other works include one in which, with pen and brush, he follows spring on its journey north from Skåne to North Cape, and one which looks at man's impact on the landscape, from the Stone Age to the present day and beyond.

JAN DANIELSON – Nature reporter for many years on the radio programme *Naturmorgon* and well-known as a presenter of the television programme *Mitt i Naturen*. Lecturer, writer and newspaper columnist. Writes about nature and the environment for the evening paper *Aftonbladet*, with a page of his own in its Sunday edition. Vice-chairman of the Swedish section of Green Cross International, a voluntary organization working for both peace and the environment. Books include a series covering the four seasons.

ROLF EDBERG (1912-97) – Author, ambassador, county governor, newspaper editor, politician. For the last three decades of his life he concentrated on writing, and was esteemed for his ability to combine scientific knowledge with a passion for the environment and defending the threatened planet Earth. He published numerous works, including *On the Shred of a Cloud* (1969), *To Live on Earth's Terms* (1974), *At the Foot of the Tree* (1974) and *And the Sea Never Rests* (1995), the latter in collaboration with the photographer Hans Strand. His piece for this book on Djurö National Park (p. 35) was one of the last nature essays he wrote.

STEFAN EDMAN – Biologist, columnist, environmental debater in the press and on radio and television, and the author of some fifteen books on nature and the environment, including *Bondens landskap* ("The farmer's landscape", 1988), *The Environment – A Common Challenge* (1990) and *Gläntor* ("Glades", 1997). Environmental training consultant to companies and local authorities, currently also personal environmental adviser to the Swedish Prime Minister.

KERSTIN EKMAN – Author with some twenty books to her name. Began as a mystery writer in the 1950s, before making her breakthrough with the novel *Mörker och blåbärsris* ("Darkness and bilberry sprigs", 1972), followed by a widely noted tetralogy beginning with *Häxringarna* ("Witches' circles", 1974). Later works include *Blackwater* (1995), for which she won the Nordic Council Literature Prize. In 1978 she was elected a member of the Swedish Academy, a position from which she later resigned. Her piece on Skuleskogen (p. 95) is an extract from *Rövarna i Skuleskogen* (1988), published by kind permission of the author and Albert Bonniers Förlag; the English version is an adaptation from a translation of the novel, with the working title "The Forest Outlaws" currently being prepared by Anna Paterson.

CLAES GRUNDSTEN – Nature photographer, travel writer and author of several books on mountain areas, including guidebooks on the Kungsleden trail, photographic works and practical guides for hikers and nature photographers. Travels widely around the globe. A physical geographer and prominent expert on the Scandinavian mountain range, he headed the Environmental Protection Agency's major survey of mountain areas in the 1980s. Author of the Agency's first national parks book, the best-selling *National Parks in Sweden* (1983).

PETER HANNEBERG – Biologist, writer, photographer and journalist specializing in nature, travel and the environment. Editor of the Environmental Protection Agency's international magazine *Enviro* since 1990. Has published a number of books on e.g. ecotourism, Swedish mountains and rivers, and the Seychelles. Chair of WWF's Ecotourism Project 1993-96. Member of the EU group of experts for the European Prize for Tourism and the Environment and of the board of the Seychelles Islands Foundation, which manages two World Heritage Sites in the Indian Ocean.

ROLF LÖFGREN – National parks expert at the Environmental Protection Agency's Natural Resources Department. Author of the report *National Parks Plan for Sweden* (1989), which forms the basis for current work on the country's national parks. Works with the establishment of new national parks and nature reserves. Project leader for a study on montane forests (1984). The Agency's expert on World Natural Heritage Sites and editor of the book *The Laponian Area* (1996).

JENS WAHLSTEDT – Writer with nature as his speciality, photographer, and an expert guide on nature tours in both the Swedish archipelagos and the tropics. Ornithologist and a pioneer of ornithological activities on Haparanda Sandskär. Secretary-General of WWF-Sweden, 1985-95, chairman of the Swedish Ecotourism Association 1996–97, and chairman of the Swedish Ornithological Society since 1997. Has published several books, including *I pandans tecken* ("In the sign of the panda", 1996) and *Öar* ("Islands", 1997).

Further reading

AN ENORMOUS NUMBER of books, reports and articles have been written about Sweden's national parks. This means that the choice is excitingly wide in every sphere of interest, but also that it is difficult to make a meaningful selection for a short list of suggestions for further reading. The best recommendation is a 386-page bibliography which offers a comprehensive survey of existing literature on the national parks, published by the Swedish Environmental Protection Agency in 1994: *Report 4280: "Documentation on the national parks of Sweden—Part 1. Bibliography"* (in Swedish). This volume, compiled by Anders Bergquist and Jan A. G. Lundquist, presents around 2,200 titles, including a number of scientific reports in English and German, grouped according to the national park concerned. The following is a brief outline of the vast array of material that has been written about our national parks.

We can begin a long time ago, with the travellers of the 18th and 19th centuries, before national parks had even been thought of. An obvious example is Linnaeus, whose account of his journey to Öland includes a description of Blå Jungfrun, and whose *Lachesis Lapponica, or a Tour in Lapland* depicts the landscape and vegetation of the Padjelanta area.

Those wishing to read about the impressions and discoveries of visitors in the early years of the 20th century will find a host of scientific articles written by botanists, zoologists, entomologists, glaciologists and geographers after the first national parks had been established in 1909, and particularly from the 1920s on. Some of these scholars had an ability to look at nature with both a scientific and a poetic eye, making their reports entertaining reading today. More popular accounts of hiking tours and other travels were also published, for example by Sten Selander and Karl-Erik Forsslund, who are quoted a number of times in this book.

Artists and literary authors made their mark, too. The caricaturist Albert Engström painted and wrote books about his beloved Gotska Sandön, as well as penning articles calling for it to be declared a national park. Scientists who entered the debate included Lars-Gunnar Romell, who as early as the 1930s criticized the way Ängsö had for a long time been allowed to become overgrown, despite the fact that it was man and his livestock that had made the island worth protecting in the first place.

After the Second World War, there was an upsurge in activity in every area—research, nature conservation, tourism and outdoor recreation. In the 1950s and 1960s a flood of scientific descriptions appeared, such as Sten Selander's studies of vegetation, Kai-Curry Lindahl's and Carl Odlitz's books on ecology and scenery, and Ernst Manker's on Sami history.

The 1970s and 1980s were to be the decades of nature books lavishly illustrated with colour photographs, with Edvin Nilsson's books on Sarek pointing the way. As part of the national physical planning process, resources on the conservation side were devoted to inventories of natural sites and features, particularly in the mountains. Reports and maps dealing with their physical geography and landforms were published, e.g. Gunnar Hoppe and Olle Melander. The Environmental Protection Agency, set up in 1967 and responsible for the national parks from 1976 on, conducted a major survey of Sweden's mountain regions, headed by Claes Grundsten. Studies were published by the Agency on areas further south which were already or were to become national parks, such as Store Mosse, Tiveden, Skuleskogen and Stenshuvud. Management plans were drawn up.

In the field of outdoor recreation, particularly recreation in mountain areas, articles were written as early as the last decade of the 19th century, thanks to the newly founded Swedish Touring Club (STF). STF's yearbooks included enthusiastic accounts of H. N. Pallin's ascents of the Sarek and Kebnekaise mountains, for Guides for hikers, such as Axel Hamberg's on Sarek (1922), also appeared. STF and the Swedish Society for the Conservation of Nature (SNF) are two NGOs which have watched over the development and interests of tourism and nature conservation, respectively, throughout the 20th century and continue to do so as we approach the millennium.

In 1989 the Environmental Protection Agency published its *"National Parks Plan for Sweden"*, with its vision of future parks, based on new data on Sweden's natural assets. In 1988–95 Claes Grundsten published a three-volume illustrated guide to the Kungsleden trail, followed by a series of guidebooks in pocket format. Tore Abrahamsson published a guidebook on the Sarek area. The Environmental Protection Agency continues to produce colourful leaflets on all the parks, reports, management plans, inventories, and illustrated books on individual parks of particular interest to the public. Some of this material is published in English.

Key to maps

Besökscenter	Visitor centre
Bro/broar	Bridge(s)
Domänreservat	Crown forest reserve
Fågelskydd	Bird sanctuary
Fornborg	Ancient fort
Naturreservat	Nature reserve
Östersjön	Baltic Sea
Tillträdesförbud	Access prohibited
— hela året	— all year round
— 15/3–31/7	— 15 March–31 July (etc.)

* Footnote, page 96:
In Kerstin Ekman's personal account of the vegetation of the Skuleskogen forest, the Swedish plant names have been 'translated' as literally as possible. To set the botanical record straight, the correct English names in the asterisked and following paragraphs are: herb Robert and herb Paris, baneberry, common stinkhorn and lesser bladderwort; wood sorrel, bracken, dwarf cornel, angular Solomon's seal and water avens, meadow-sweet and alpine sowthistle; star sedge and goldenrod, great mullein, bog rosemary, chickweed wintergreen and toothwort; hard fern and mountain melick, wood meadow-grass and rough horsetail.

Photographers

THE PHOTOGRAPHS IN this book are the work of the photographers listed below. Where several photographs appear on one page, they are listed from top to bottom and from left to right, first the left hand side of the page, followed by the middle and right hand side.

Front cover:
Hans Strand (Rapadalen, Sarek).

Back cover:
Hans Strand (view of Skierfe, Sarek);
Claes Grundsten/Bildhuset (Ängsö);
Jörgen Wiklund/N (great grey owl);
Peter Hanneberg/TioFoto (Blå Jungfrun).

1 Hans Strand (Akkatjåkkå, Sarek).
4 Peter Hanneberg/TioFoto.
5 Per-Olov Eriksson/N.
8 Björn Svensson/Myra.
10 Klas Rune/N.
13 Jan Schützer/N.
14 Hans Strand.
16 Anders Ekholm/TioFoto.
18 Tomas Utsi/Myra.
 Tore Hagman/N.
19 Jan-Peter Lahall.
 Lars Johansson/IBL.
 Jarl von Scheele/Pressens Bild.
 Mats Rosenberg/TioFoto.
20 Staffan Arvegård/N.
21 Fjällfoto/IBL.
22 Staffan Arvegård/N.
23 Peter Dyballa/Myra,
 Tommy Bergström,
 Per-Olov Eriksson/N,
 Tore Hagman/N,
 Heinz Schrempp/IBL.
24 Jan-Peter Lahall.
25 Jan-Peter Lahall.
26 Bruno Helgesson/N
 Peter Hanneberg/TioFoto.
27 Staffan Arvegård/N,
 Ola Jennersten/N,
 Peter Hanneberg/TioFoto,
 Anders Geidemark/N (black guillemot).
28 Åke Lindau/IBL.
29 Ingmar Holmåsen/N.
30 Sven Halling/Naturbild.
31 Åke Lindau/IBL,
 Björn Svensson/Myra,
 Klas Rune/N,
 Jan Grahn/N.
32 Jan Töve/N.
33 Hans Kongbäck/N.
34 Jan Töve/N,
 Mattias Klum/TioFoto.
35 Tore Hagman/N.
36 Jan Töve/N.
37 Janos Jurka/N,
 Lennart Mathiasson/N,
 Torbjörn Lija/N,
 Ulf Sjöstedt/TioFoto,
 Bengt Ekman/N.
38 Jan-Peter Lahall.

39 Alf Linderheim/N.
40 Jan-Peter Lahall.
41 Lennart Mathiasson/N,
 Jan-Peter Lahall,
 Jarl von Scheéle//Pressens Bild,
 Ola Jennersten/N.
42 Klas Rune/N.
43 Klas Rune/N.
44 Peter Hanneberg/TioFoto.
45 Klas Rune/N,
 Peter Hanneberg/TioFoto,
 Peter Hanneberg/TioFoto.
46 Peter Hanneberg/TioFoto.
47 Hans Nelsäter/Bildarkivet,
 Klas Rune/N,
 Klas Rune/N,
 Åke Lindau/IBL.
48 Jan-Peter Lahall,
 Björn-Eyvind Swahn/N.
49 Bengt Hedberg/Naturbild,
 Ulf Risberg/N,
 Peter Hanneberg/TioFoto,
 Peter Hanneberg/TioFoto,
 Bengt Hedberg/Naturbild.
50 Håkan Hjort/N.
52 Klas Rune/N,
 Ulf Risberg/N.
53 Bengt Hedberg/Naturbild,
 Ola Jennersten/N,
 Alf Linderheim/N,
 Per-Olov Eriksson/N.
54 Pär Domeij/Bildsmedjan.
56 Jens Wahlstedt,
 Jens Wahlstedt.
57 Jonas Forsberg,
 Peter Fredman.
58 Jan-Peter Lahall.
59 Torbjörn Lilja/N,
 Klas Rune/N,
 Börje Hjortborg/Norrlandia,
 Börje Olsson/Norrlandia,
 Sven Halling/Naturbild.
60 Jörgen Wiklund/N.
61 Claes Grundsten/Bildhuset.
62 Claes Grundsten/Bildhuset.
63 Tomas Utsi/Myra.
64 Pär Domeij/Bildsmedjan,
 Håkan Hjort/N.
65 Claes Grundsten/Bildhuset,
 Torbjörn Lilja/N,
 Sixten Jonsson/N,
 Jörgen Wiklund/N.
66 Claes Grundsten/Bildhuset.
67 Alf Linderheim/N.
68 Hans Strand,
 Bruno Helgesson/N.
69 Lennart Mathiasson/N,
 Per-Olov Eriksson/N.
70 Sten Gustafsson/Myra:
71 Henry Andreasson/Pressens Bild,
 Alf Linderheim/N,
 Bengt Ekman/N,
 Erling Schön/N,
 Ola Jennersten/N.
72 Kate Kärrberg/Naturbild.
73 Leif Östergren/Myra.

74 Claes Grundsten/Bildhuset.
76 Claes Grundsten/Bildhuset.
77 Tore Hagman/N,
 Kate Kärrberg/Naturbild.
78 Kate Kärrberg/Naturbild.
79 Jan Rietz/TioFoto,
 Ola Jennersten/N,
 Claes Grundsten/Bildhuset,
 Bengt Hedberg/Naturbild,
 Peter Hanneberg/TioFoto.
80 Jan Schützer/N.
81 Jörgen Wiklund/N.
82 Lennart Broborn/N,
 Edvin Nilsson/N.
83 Stefan Rosengren/Naturbild,
 Jan Schützer/N,
 Jan Grahn/N (dotterel),
 Hans Nelsäter/Bildarkivet.
84 Claes Grundsten/Bildhuset.
86 Tore Hagman/N,
 Thore Johansson/Myra.
87 Håkan Hjort/N,
 Tor Lundberg/N.
88 Claes Grundsten/Bildhuset.
90 Hans Strand.
91 Roland Svensson/Bildarkivet,
 Claes Grundsten/Bildhuset,
 Bengt Lundberg/N,
 Kenneth Johansson/Myra.
92 Jan-Peter Lahall.
93 Jan Töve/N.
94 Claes Grundsten/Bildhuset.
95 Bengt Ekman/N,
 Jan-Peter Lahall.
96 Erling Schön/N,
 Hans Nelsäter/Bildarkivet.
97 Tore Häggström/Norrlandia,
 Jan Grahn/N,
 Alf Linderheim/N,
 Jan Schützer/N.
98 Erling Schön/N.
99 Anders Good/IBL.
100 Klas Rune/N.
101 Jan Töve/N,
 Torbjörn Arvidsson/TioFoto.
102 Jan-Peter Lahall.
103 Klas Rune/N.
104 Klas Rune/N.
105 Claes Grundsten/Bildhuset,
 Peter Hanneberg/TioFoto,
 Torbjörn Arvidsson/TioFoto,
 Bengt Hedberg/Naturbild,
 Tomas Gustavsson/Pressens Bild.
106 Håkan Hjort/N.
108 Tor Lundberg/N,
 Anders Ekholm/TioFoto.
109 Tor Lundberg/N,
 Håkan Hjort/N,
 Staffan Widstrand/Naturbild,
 Håkan Hjort/N.
110 Torbjörn Skogedal/Myra.
112 Jan Schützer/N.
113 Tapani Räsänen/Naturbild,
 Leif Gustavsson/Myra.
114 Claes Grundsten/Bildhuset.
115 Christer Fredriksson/Naturbild,

 Jonas Forsberg/N,
 Janos Jurka/N,
 Lennart Mathiasson/N.
116 Kenneth Johansson/Myra.
117 Klas Rune/N.
118 Claes Grundsten/Bildhuset.
119 Sven Gillsäter/TioFoto,
 Jan Grahn/N,
 Göran Ekström/TioFoto,
 Torbjörn Lilja/N.
120 Claes Grundsten/Bildhuset.
121 Erling Schön/N.
122 Alf Linderheim/N,
 Peter Hanneberg/TioFoto.
123 Jan-Peter Lahall.
124 Jörgen Wiklund/N,
 Peter Hanneberg/TioFoto.
125 Peter Hanneberg/TioFoto,
 Peter Hanneberg/TioFoto,
 Peter Rolén/Norrlandia,
 JanPeter Lahall.
126 Jan Grahn/N.
127 Jan-Peter Lahall.
128 Jan-Peter Lahall.
129 Bruno Helgesson/N,
 Erling Schön/N,
 Folke Hårrskog/N,
 Stjärnfoto/IBL.
130 Claes Grundsten/Bildhuset.
131 Dan Motun/Myra.
132 Ove Eriksson/TioFoto.
133 Lars Dahlström/TioFoto,
 Claes Grundsten/Bildhuset.
135 Rolf Löfgren,
 Claes Grundsten/Bildhuset,
 Peter Hanneberg/TioFoto,
 Anders Järnmark/Myra.
136 Claes Grundsten/Bildhuset.
137 Sten Gustafsson/Myra,
 Bruno Helgesson/N.
138 Claes Grundsten/Bildhuset,
 Claes Grundsten/Bildhuset.
139 Lennart Mathiasson/N,
 Jesper Sandström/Pressens Bild,
 Claes Grundsten/Bildhuset,
 Lennart Mathiasson/N,
 Jan Töve/N.
140 Håkan Hjort/N.
141 Jan Schützer/N,
 Jan Grahn/N.
142 Tomas Utsi/Myra,
 Peter Ugander/N.
143 Bengt Ekman/N,
 Tore Abrahamsson/TioFoto,
 Henrik Ekman/N,
 Tomas Utsi/Myra.
144 Claes Grundsten/Bildhuset.
145 Peter Hanneberg/TioFoto.
146 Claes Grundsten/Bildhuset.
147 Bengt Hedberg/Naturbild,
 Eddie Granlund/Naturbild.
148 Roine Karlsson/Pressens Bild.
149 Bengt Hedberg/Naturbild,
 Jan Töve/N,
 Alf Linderheim/N,
 Klas Rune/N.